Esoteric Apprentice

New and Enlarged

(Incorporating 2025 and The World Teacher)

STEVEN CHERNIKEEFF

To
Robert and Peter

Acknowledgments

I would like to thank all of those many participants in the Twelves Group who, over the years, believed, experienced and manifested Twelves. Without you, and your sacrifices, it would not have happened. Respect and love.

Particular thanks go to my dear friends and co-workers Robert Adams and Dr. Peter Maslin who represented the core triangle and travelled with me on this glorious and mysterious journey until they were called home.

Thanks, and much appreciation goes to Mindy Burge who has held my hand through the publication process and editing and has become a true friend of Twelves. Additional thanks also go to Heather Olalde for assisting with the editing process. Thanks also goes to Phillip Lindsay, Stephane Chollet, Patrick Chouinard and many others for their reviews and friendship over the years. Comrades in Arms are they.

Thanks to all the co-workers in Twelves who have joined with me to take up the Banner once more.

Thank you to Duane Carpenter for permission to use the beautiful Twelves mandala on the cover.

Respect and loving appreciation to Helena P. Blavatsky, Alice A. Bailey and Helena and Nicholas Roerich, for they lit the fire from which we all warm ourselves.

Last, but not least, my appreciation, love, and respect must go to The Initiate who guided us through the labyrinth of our egos to the synthesis of group work (as far as we could achieve it).

Table of Contents

Introduction

As I approached the shoreline, I was certain that the journey had taken me far from home. We never remember much, of course, about our life before birth nor the issues or future challenges we bring with us. Nor do we know the complications, experiences, or what is expected of us, here and now. Or do we? Is our current life full of shambles and chaos? Or is our karma engraved into our souls prior to birth our future steps chosen in advance and pre-plotted, often with other opportunities laid out, considered, and planned?

Those of us who have experienced, at least a partial, awakening are part of a huge vista of endeavour that slowly transforms our planet from dullard to genius, from the unreal to the real. There is a vast cosmic turning of the karmic clock as it tick-tocks its way to growth and enlightenment. If we can accept that we are a part of this unveiling and transformation of the greater whole, then this must also be true of our present incarnation, which is indelibly linked to everything around us, circumstances, people, the environment, etc.

Our daily experience as we climb, slowly, the footpath of knowledge before each and every one of us contributes to this larger evolution. We cannot be separate and apart, although we may feel like that sometimes, as however small our contribution, our drop is still part of the ocean.

Right now, collectively, we are a part of what is known as the externalization or, in other words, the unveiling of those at the heart of human evolution (the Masters of the Wisdom--to use the Theosophical term--are people who have achieved enlightenment and have taken the fifth initiation. They work to aid humanity) this will happen when humanity has matured enough to understand and accept the wisdom that the Masters have given humanity down the ages.

Many are involved in this Great Endeavour in all branches of human life. Sciences, Arts, Philosophies, Religions and all those things in-between will be rarefied. There are Masters and Initiates and those working towards self-evolution in all those branches and more.

That is not to say that these great humans recognize they are a part of the externalization—most are oblivious—yet they are integral to it as much as that drop in the Ocean.

There are some who have chosen before birth to work directly with those forces of evolution to undertake specific work for this externalisation. This does not make these individuals greater or lesser than the rest of us but a part of the same mix. In one life they might decide to work anonymously unaware, even to themselves, that they are part of this greater whole and in another be a conscious part of the process. This all depends on their individual karma and that incarnation's purpose.

Thus, we have this collection of souls working at various levels and in various capacities for a united intention. So, now let us leave aside this flow of incarnation slowly traversing through the world's karma, national karma, family karma and individual karma and focus on what this book is about, where it is going and any lessons that may be learnt for future group active meditative service work.

This book is not fiction. It is a story and a re-telling of events that occurred, but neither is it a claim for anything. It gives one person's experience, as it happened and is recounted as truthfully as it is possible to do so.

Naturally, no one is perfect, and if I have erred at all from the recounting, then I apologise in advance.

The work continues. This is a personal recount of the experiment that we undertook in group work as sentient aspirants and disciples working consciously with a group of Masters and Initiates on the inner planes. I shall retell the whys, wherefores, and how's as best as I can so that it might benefit future efforts and I shall not avert my mind to avoid including our failures for it is from those from which we gain the most.

Some of those that travelled with us are still here and some have returned home. It was not an easy task that we had before us but many of us consider it to be the very pinnacle of our esoteric life here together and it rests in our consciousness, nudging us from time to time with its familiar melodic refrain.

So, come with us on our journey, a journey with mistakes, egos, misunderstandings and, yes, successes as we were tried in the fire of the inner ashram. This work was designed to cooperate, consciously, with the forces of reconstruction and change that are sweeping through our planet and to do so in magnified group formation.

I decided early on not to write a thesis on the experience with quotations strewn on every page (even though my academic training would have made this somewhat easier) but rather free flow, although, the majority of everything here written could be supported by the works of the three great esoteric initiates: Helena Petrovna Blavatsky, Alice Ann Bailey and Helena Roerich.

I know that the experiences that we had, as a group, were more likened to the intuition and soul contact than any book work and I wanted to avoid justifying the work we did with heavy quotations. It is enough to say that these three great initiates laid the foundations for all of us to follow. I have, then, only made limited quotations, within the text itself, when it was absolutely necessary. Further study of the books by these three initiates is strongly advised.

Suffice it to say that contact was made, and some instructions were given by an Initiate within the ashram (we will call him The Initiate from now on); precise guidelines were laid out for us to follow.

The only promise made was that there was no promise. It was an experiment. The instruction was through soul impression/higher telepathy via the same methodology as Helena Petrovna Blavatsky, Alice Ann Bailey and Helena Roerich, as previously mentioned.

I shall start at the very beginning with my younger experiences which will place into context that which follows. Follow us, then, upon this journey of discovery and think there on that here was a group that tried, was tested and laid one of the foundation stones for future group service work.

Importantly, it should be mentioned at the very beginning, this work was physically present, not virtual or absent. This distinguishes it from the vast majority of other group service work that is undertaken as service work to enhance the externalisation process. There was a specific purpose to this early training and laying of foundations.

This book sets out the journey, describes the background and importance of Twelves and working in Groups of Twelve and lays out the process that was undertaken. May it be of use in future years.

Note. The work of Twelves is very much linked to the Hierarchal Conclave in 2025 and so large sections of the book *2025 and The World Teacher* have been incorporated into this new and enlarged edition.

"We are all Embers in the Fire of the One."

The Initiate May 1982

Chapter One

---ᗒ◦ᗕ---

Early Days

"DO THINGS BEGIN when we are born?" asked the small boy.

"Not at all," smiled the old man. "Not at all. Long, long before you were born things began and things will unfold like a roll of silk unravelled upon a marbled floor.

A rejected child at 6 weeks old and raised in a Baptist children's home was scant preparation for what was to come… or so I thought.

It started in an upstairs bedroom of the home. Always a different child who liked to sleep with a long stick under his bed (it was a spear in a previous existence, he would say) the shock of the luminous colour was the first inkling of the destiny to follow. Lying motionless atop the bed then moving to go off on some task elsewhere, the feet were still there, but in a luminous green. This was the first shock, but no one believed it nor cared about a little boy's ramblings about his feet in shining green on the bed.

It was a Baptist home and such oddities were dismissed as childish fantasy. It was even stranger, the little boy pondered, that people seemed to have colours surrounding them. When he put his hands in front of his face then withdrew them, the hands remained distinctly where they

1

were yet in this haunting, luminous green. But even these oddities did not prepare him for what was to come and the disturbances it would bring as, the problem would reveal itself, only he could see and hear these oddities.

The Bell (or gong) was the strangest thing. When first heard, I assumed it was some sort of a ship, in the far distance, and as I lived beside the sea this assumption was not quite so odd as it first appeared. The strangeness became, well, stranger when others were asked why the Bell kept sounding at about ten seconds intervals. I could hear it in my room and whilst walking the street. Others simply looked at me and said, "What

Bell?" And as was the habit of those that ran the home, they would simply ignore my questions.

And then he came, Charles the TV repair man, that is. Now, Charles would get involved in discussions with my foster mother (although I was never actually fostered, but let's ignore the technicality as that's what she called herself) concerning Christianity, saving souls and the like. I would listen in a bit (I was around 15 or 16 years old at the time). Then it happened. The conversation arrived at, "Was it possible or right to seek communication with someone who had died?"

You see, Charles was a Christian Spiritualist and my foster mother was determined to save him (she had probably given up with me). They actually agreed on many things, funnily enough, but not on the fundamental premise that communication with the dead was possible or, indeed, warranted

One side trying to express the idea that not only was it possible but to be encouraged, mostly to comfort the grieving and bring knowledge, and the other explaining that it was the work of the Devil and so, it can be seen, they had some way to go to reach agreement. After this exchange, which ended comfortably enough with a smile from Charles and an exhaustive sigh from the foster mother I managed to engage Charles, whilst he tried to fix my record player (yes, he fixed those as well), in conversation.

"Charles?" I asked, quizzically, "What is this Christian Spiritualist thing about?" Charles then began to tell me, with a zeal that befits someone telling an open secret--an afterlife does exist. As he did so, I enquired more and more. "What happens then?" I asked, and "What is the purpose?"

Then it was revealed. He talked about the seven planes of existence, and I knew I was receiving something very special.

I asked Charles if I could come to the church (that's what they called them, but I doubt many churches are overjoyed with such a connection), but he was very concerned about the impact on the foster mother's zeal.

However, eager was I, and so he invited me to attend the service with him the following Sunday.

It seemed strange to me that the service mimicked, almost, the services I was forced to attend at the local Baptist church. The obvious difference was that there was always someone there who would select people from the audience then relay messages from the dead, mostly innocuous and bland, but that was not the point.

The foundation of going along on Sundays was to set me off for decades to come. Although after a relatively short time I would leave the very nice Christian Spiritualists behind, I have never forgotten they were my entry point, and I am fond of them to this day. And, let's not forget, there was that ubiquitous Bell.

Bong, silence, Bong, silence, Bong, silence—it would go and then stop for a few hours. Then the sequence would repeat. It was unsettling, to say the least. By that time, I had given up asking people around me if they could hear it. The answer was always, "No, you are imagining it." All, of course, except those dear old Christian Spiritualists, who, although they could not hear it, tried to give me an explanation that it was the Astral Bell (referred to in A.P. Sinnet's *Occult World*), but the Christian Spiritualists explanation was far more mundane.

The Astral Bell, I was informed, was rung upon the astral plane, obviously, but no one knew quite why that was; it seemed it was some sort of homing device. Even this rather simplistic explanation (the Christian Spiritualist's explanation, not Sinnet's) was rather better than the, "It doesn't exist" one proffered by those normal people who live in a very different paradigm.

Then there were the colours, of course, but that was more satisfactorily explained as the human aura (even Christians have their halos and their Saints have a distinctive glow in those old master paintings that might indicate auric presence). The Christian Spiritualists didn't quite know what to do with this 16-year-old boy who hovered around on Sundays. One even told me to go and concentrate on life and career and come back to pondering life after death questions when I was nearer to it! I thought this strange advice, as we never know when we are near or far from it, I explained--much to the slight discomfort of the very dear and kind old Spiritualist who had invited me to tea after the Sunday service.

I remember that I started to visit the old second-hand bookshops and go straight to the Occult section. I had begun to acquire Spiritualist-inclined books and attend the odd Spiritualist Church. Eventually, as I found the Christian segment a bit too limiting—it seemed to me they wanted to have their cake and eat it too, as they believed in the right to communicate with those who have passed and yet did not quite want to give up their Christian upbringings—I moved on.

I joined the Spiritualist Association of Great Britain (I guess technically I'm still a member as I purchased a lifetime membership, which was available back then), and I travelled to London for several visits, sittings, and Saturday lectures on everything from auras to Egyptian Temple Dancing. From various mediums and presenters came more simplistic explanations of the Bell and colours, which had died down considerably at this stage. To be fair, it did lead me away from the basic and the fundamental, as my focus was far more drawn to the philosophy and meaning of what had gone and what was before us than to any chats with the dead.

I discovered Ursula Roberts's book *Hints on Spiritual Unfoldment*, which had a huge impact on me back then, as it introduced to me the heart of the Spiritualist philosophy, which was much more important to me than a message from Uncle Fred that he was ok in the land of the sun. Also, I started to study Silver Birch books and, eventually, White Eagle. All of these tomes were useful, and I devoured stacks of them, but something was still missing.

I knew of the fundamental message of life after death, the simple explanations of what happens after you die. I knew, intuitively and simplistically, that this was true and right; however, there must be MORE. For the first time, I started to feel like I was on the very end of a long rubber band and the invisible hand that held me at one end had let go. I was travelling very fast, but I knew not where.

1975 was my *anno excitatio* (year of awakening). Seventeen was a young age to be spending considerable time looking around second-hand bookshops (the Bell and colours had all but stopped, thank goodness).

I remember well when I alighted upon an odd, boring looking book, yellow in colour—*The Reappearance of the Christ*, it said on the cover, but it was in the Occult section. I was intrigued and made my purchase.

This book wasn't the first Alice A. Bailey book I read, but it sparked my interest, so I bought *Initiation, Human and Solar* and *A Treatise on White Magic* in quick succession. I then read *Initiation, Human and Solar* as my very first Theosophical work. I contacted Jan Nation at Lucis Trust and received a plethora of free material to devour. I had the pleasure of meeting Jan, the first time in 1977 when I was nineteen, then several times later, at the annual Festival for Mind Body Spirit in London. I was very impressed that Jan always remembered me, greeting me by name each year. What a joy she was, and I owe her a debt of gratitude for putting up with my many questions.

In this way, I discovered the esoteric teachings of the Master Djwhal Khul (more commonly referred to as DK) and of Helena Petrovna Blavatsky's (H.P.B.) work and, later, through my dear friend Robert Adams, the teachings of Nicholas and Helena Roerich and *Agni Yoga*.

I went along to a market in London (Camden I think) and bought the whole set from a market trader whom, I assume, like most of us, had a double life, but that was where you purchased the Agni Yoga books back in those days.

I would meet every Saturday with Robert, a founder member and core triangle member of the Twelves Work, and discuss esotericism, philosophy, and theosophy, delving through the pages of his extensive bedroom library (of which I was entirely envious, I'm ashamed to say).

I was on a collection spree, replacing my Spiritualist collection with a Theosophical one. I had found, I thought at the time, a higher form than Spiritualism, and I shed my previous fixation step by step.

At this point, though, I would like to pay tribute to the Spiritualist movement, as it brought me, and probably thousands of others, into the esoteric teachings which are the bedrock of the Divine Mysteries. But leave it behind I must, I thought, as I began the intense study and meditation that would lead me later to the experiment.

Robert, who I had met through the local new age grapevine, as we both lived fairly near each other, had a garden shed that he had turned into a meditation studio.

Wallpapered, incense-laden, filled with Buddha statues, we spent many hours in there honing our meditation skills every Saturday, followed by a sumptuous dinner cooked by his lovely parents (adopted parents, I would learn later) who were quite bemused by Robert and I as we spent so many hours in that shed and his bedroom discussing the finer points of Theosophical thinking.

Robert had Hodgkin's disease and would later pass away before reaching the age of 40, but not before we grew to be great friends and not before our meditation had led us to another pathway, a surprising and some-times shocking pathway, that would lead to us working closely together over many years as the experiment was unveiled to us piece by piece.

This was a difficult process, unnerving too, but we never wavered in our intent to see it through once we knew that we were being asked to participate in a group service meditation experiment. At first, we were incredulous, confused, and almost disbelieving.

At the point of midnight 31st December 1981, a mysterious stranger approached and spoke to me; Robert felt it too, the whole cabin was electrified.

No name was given, just some words and a symbol:

"Find the point within the Triangle Divine – when this has been achieved you will learn more."

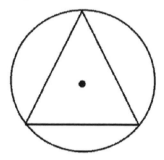

We internally knew that we had something to do but were obviously unsure what, how, or why. We only knew we had made contact, and thus we went through a glamorous stage, as so many do, particularly of a youthful disposition, where we felt we were on a mission and had direct contact with a Master. In fact, we eventually learnt a timely lesson in humility which stayed with us through the years of work we would undertake together and with the many others from all over the world. Masters often, and normally do, work through their Initiates.

Over-identification with a Master's energy often is attributed, as we did, as direct contact person to person. What I can say, unequivocally now, and that we learnt back in the 80s, was that we had direct contact with an Initiate from the ashram known as the Brotherhood of the Star (an ashramic amalgamation of those who work to bring the Externalisation of the Hierarchy about) and the inner, esoteric core behind Krishnamurti's work with the Order of the Star. We had learnt the glamour and trap, which we should all avoid, of associating the vast energy of a Master and his ashram with a personal relationship.

As Krishnamurti is here mentioned this is a good pause so that his work, with the Order of the Star, might be explained a little further as it does link-in to the work we undertook later as the Twelves Group. Krishnamurti, as the common legend goes, had an organisation created by Annie Besant, C.W Leadbeater and others to enable him to function as the vehicle of the Christ (an office within the Spiritual Hierarchy rather than an individual) but, as we know, it was disbanded it in 1929 and he declared, "Truth is a pathless land".

It is my contention that it was the Christ who withdrew His energy from the Krishnamurti experiment (please see Addendum) that led to the Order being disbanded, not the other way around. This is an important difference; however, the outcome was the same. Christ (the office and the being) had decided to Reappear Himself and not through another human vehicle. It is recommended that readers study the books of Alice A. Bailey for more information regarding the Hierarchal externalisation program.

As Robert and I continued our meditation work, we received further instruction and the invitation to undertake work in twelve formation and to act as a conduit for Hierarchical ashramic energy, as an experiment and expansion of the triangles work hither too undertaken by Lucis Trust and others. Also, the latest expansion from the proposed work of 'organons', work in groups of nine, as outlined by John R. Sinclair in his book *The Other Universe*. In fact, John was a personal friend of Robert's and was kept up to date with our work with the Twelves Group over the years.

To quote John:

"It is suggested that a membership of nine is a particularly useful organic group structure. It is not too large... on the other hand it is large enough to subdivide into three groups of three should special concentration on components of a project be necessary."

When we first formed our group, it was known as Lodge of the Star, as we had been informed of our lineage to Krishnamurti's time and we decided to honour that link.

However, as we proceeded over the years, it became obvious that the group had been set up for one purpose only--the experiment, in Groups of Twelve people, that was to have a direct link and connection to the ashram and to act as a conduit and so we decided to change the group's name to Twelves Group, as that better reflected the groups purpose.

The Master Morya (often referred to simply as M.) in the book *Agni Yoga* had mentioned working in Groups of Twelve back in 1929 (the year of Krishnamurti's disbanding of the Order of the Star):

"137. People do not want to understand group work, which multiplies the forces. The dodecahedron is one of the most perfect structures, with a dynamic power that can resist many assaults. A group of twelve, systematically united, truly can master even cosmic events. It must be understood that the enlarging of such a group can weaken it, undermining the dynamic force of its structure."

At the time, we had not stumbled across this passage by M. but it clearly foretells the work we would undertake together. The group slowly attracted to itself members who had felt drawn to its work, mostly through their own meditation. That's how Dr. Peter Maslin joined us (Peter was a doctor on the Isle of Lewis in Scotland and a great student of Alice Bailey, probably one of the best read I have ever known. His Bailey collection was threadbare with the amount of study he undertook). Peter would grow to become one of the inner triangle that ran the group. Peter brought a real discipline to the group, although most of us could not rise every 4am, as he did, to meditate for hours (normally outside in the garden), but he added much to our group work and was with us for the long haul over many years. Peter moved down

South so that he could be physically near our work. Peter was a rock.

It became clearer that getting twelve people together was not the real challenge but finding twelve disciplined disciples became an issue every year and each time we organised Gatherings (Gatherings were where members would attend physically to actually undertake the group formation work). Normally these were held annually and were held in Glastonbury, England, but others were held at Findhorn, Scotland, in London, and in New York.

Each year it was expensive for our European, and especially our American, members to fly over to join us, but a core did so. Sometimes some could come and others could not, and so getting a Twelve (plus one or two spares) who had the qualities needed was a headache for organisers, but we did accomplish this on many occasions (not getting twelve disciples, we never achieved that, but in holding a Twelve).

We slowly gained participants (there was no official membership, we simply gathered details of those with real interest) across the world of a couple hundred, and we produced newsletters, booklets, and leaflets. In those days it was all done by post, and, thankfully, Robert took charge of the group's organisation and did nearly all the hard work of mail-outs, organising the odd talks and typing stuff up—how easier it would be now in this age of mass, social communications!

The group was financed by donations. The group worked on and agreed upon a Vision Statement for the activities ahead, which would be at the very front of our 'Twelves Guidelines: *A Manual for Group Workers.*' This document has been added in its entirety later in the book as Chapter 6, as we felt it was important to include it as a whole, as the group had collectively written it.

Vision Statement

"Our commitment is to work in formation with groups of twelve people through Geometry of Divinity and by so doing assist those who work for the Light; to undertake Soul-infused energy work for planetary healing and transformation and closely cooperate with the Forces of Spiritual Change. Individual workers contribute within the group through harmonious blending and focussed effort."

With the Vision Statement in place and a number of publications printed and distributed, we were developing, outwardly, a small organisation that could prepare members for the actual work of Twelves.

We wanted to prepare people as much as we could before physically gathering, as it would save an enormous amount of time once we were physically present.

Yet, despite our best efforts, considerable time was spent each meeting in training and explaining, as there were nearly always new members who would be experiencing a Twelve for the first time, and, as the formation is a disciplined one and the energies we encountered very real, it was essential all participants understood, and had practiced, where they would stand.

In 1983, Robert Pitts, another prominent group member, emerged as the leader of a group of New York esotericists who wanted to work with us on the Twelves work. We agreed with Robert Pitts that formal group membership was unnecessary, as previously mentioned, and that soul quality would be the only important thing, so the Twelves Group never had formal memberships.

Robert helped us for many years bringing people over to London and Glastonbury and organising a Gathering in New York, which was attended by around 50 people, a great success despite the local fundamentalist Christians trying to stop us from using the University hall.

When Robert appeared on local radio, he was asked the question, "Is this the work of the Devil?" He answered, "Well, I don't have acquaintance with him myself." This seemed to lighten the moment, and we were allowed to hire the hall as planned and undertake our work.

This was the time, in conjunction with and, in fact leading, the outer work when we initiated our group triangles. We had, of course, many triangles working for many years at the core of the group, but we agreed that to participate in Twelves it was necessary, and compulsory, to join our triangle work prior to undertaking a Twelve.

The vast majority of the teachings given to us for the formation of the experiment were during the years 1982 to 1986. It was explained that there would be very little in addition coming after that, as our purpose was not to spread teachings, in the traditional sense, but that we were receiving them for the specific purpose of experimental Twelves only. We were told that we had all we needed and that the real work was on the inner planes.

During the year 1982, around 90% of the teachings were given. I have decided to only quote sparingly from the teachings, as this is not the focus of this book, and I was always told that it was the practical work that was important. Everything in this book follows closely the instructions as given by The Initiate, paying close heed to what we were told regarding the purpose.

The method of teaching was given through higher telepathy during ashramic meditation. Let's pause here... whether this is accepted or not is of no consequence. What is of import is was the work useful? And, might it be useful to future groups? I cannot fully answer those questions, but I, and others, believe that this group experiment was useful, and it is important to document this very real attempt to become a conduit for hierarchy through ashramic contact by dedicated disciples over a 20 year period (1980 – 2000) although there was an initial teaching period 1978 to 1980 where seed thoughts were given and recorded in a book published under the title *A Pilgrim Inspired.*

I have been asked many times if the Twelves Group will restart. I thought it very unlikely but since publication the group has re-formed. Do I think work in Twelve formation will arise again? Yes, it has, and I hope our part in its concept and development will be useful. I am happily working with the group and if we do not achieve our potential then furthers steps will have been made for future coworkers to take up the challenge.

The Work has restarted and moved from the Preparatory Stage to the Implementory Stage but, of course, we do not know how long this stage will be. Whether we start it now and it is continued by others after we are gone or if The World Teacher is among us post 2025 and we move to the third and last Stage.

"What is time, dear brothers? It is a fraction of space locked between great evolutionary events."

The Initiate July 1984

Chapter Two

Who Are You?

AH, THE ETERNAL QUESTION! But in this case who was he? --this mysterious figure who arrived on the eve of 1981/82 and introduced himself to the two budding disciples who, it must be said, were eager to serve the Hierarchy that they had so recently discovered through a myriad of books? The fact is the contact was not sought nor expected and was a pretty disturbing, mysterious, yet peaceful event. It is important to clarify, for the purpose of this book, what and who he was, as the information he conveyed set those two youthful disciples upon a decade-long quest.

A point worth mentioning here, when we say "he" this is the energy body chosen at that time and in no way suggests that the hidden realms are gender related. The soul is genderless. We all incarnate as female and male to participate in our soul's growth and development. At this time, masters take male bodies for energy reasons only.

In the early days, as a sin of youthfulness and glamour unfortunately, we both thought that the person instructing us was a Master of the Wisdom In Homine (Koot Hoomi aka K.H.). In later years we were corrected that this person was, in fact, an initiate of the ashram of Koot Hoomi.

(Henceforth this book will describe him as The Initiate and K.H. as, well, K.H.)

It is a common failing of those on the pathway to attribute greatness and grandeur; and, in particular, it is a glamour of many esotericists who conflate their importance and the importance of those they make contact with.

We were informed that to dispel this at a very early stage would have created utter confusion, so in early days we referred to The Initiate as 'K.H.' and, absurd as this may sound now, we ask forgiveness and understanding from you, dear reader. As stated, this is a common misunderstanding of energy. Ashrams are energy, and, when stepping that down, it is easily misunderstood and, even worse, misapplied. I often use the analogy of a sponge: the water (energy) entering from the Master may be pure, but the sponge of personality of the recipient always dilutes it and this is the important point, taints it with bias, colouring it with preconceived ideas and thoughts. This applies to Blavatsky, Bailey and Roerich too, although much less than myself, of course, as they were senior initiates and I am not.

Knowing this leads to real understanding and forgiveness of those parts of us which are less than perfect. Hence, I pay little attention to the personality defects of those three great initiates and to my fellow disciples treading the pathway as I recognise my own gaping weaknesses and faults. "To Err is human, to forgive is Divine," and I'd rather you concentrate on the last part if possible.

Blavatsky, Bailey, and Roerich, in part, had direct contact for a specific purpose with a Master, as they were on the teaching line and were required to produce large portions of the Ancient Wisdom as a teaching device for the masses of humanity. This was not what our group was asked to do.

The work was quite different in the sense that we were experimenting with actual, direct contact with the ashram and distribution of energy for specific purposes. Lucis Trust, of course, undertakes distributive work too, but not in the same way, nor for the same purposes, as their main focus is mass teaching, but we are all ONE endeavour.

Back to our theme which will lead, later, to the work we undertook over those two decades. The Initiate, then, connected with us only to impart that information that was useful to the group's purpose, working in Groups of Twelve (why the number twelve, particularly, is important we will discuss in the next chapter).

The methodology used was the same as with that of Blavatsky, Bailey, and Roerich, that of higher telepathy, which utilises the higher chakras and imparts a purer (not, please note, 'pure') connection. Masters often will use this method in many walks of life, not just the esoteric.

Most people will be completely unaware that this connection has taken place, but it can produce great moments in the life of humanity in the sciences, arts etc. For esotericists who are consciously on the pathway, this can be recognised, and, for a few, a conscious knowledge that this has, and will, happen is understood. It is important to note here that this does not, in any way, make those who have this conscious link any more important than those who might receive it unconsciously; it is just that this is their task at this time.

For some reason, I know not why, a few of us were asked to undertake this group work experiment and to draw to us those who could aid this work. The Initiate gave most of the ashramic information we needed during 1982, but there were additions throughout the decade until 1992 when the instructions stopped, with only very occasional contact with The Initiate, as we were told we had what was appropriate for this phase of the work. It appears The Initiate was a good time manager.

In the mid-1980s, I forget exactly when, we were visited physically by a stranger (a Chinaman/Tibetan) who purported to be from the ashram and had found Robert's house via a light on the inner planes (a star, he said) hovering over the house. I cannot confirm or deny this to be the case. I simply report it here. We dined with him and discussed several group matters, then he left, never to be seen again.

There were several other, but rare, physical manifestations which might be of some interest, but I don't want to focus on these nor deflect too much from the purpose of this book: to lay out what actually happened when a group of conscious disciples undertook to physically meet and, in group formation, connect with real, ashramic forces for purpose. The Initiate gave many instructions as to the working and set-up of twelves group work and gave several tools, but the most important of these were manifested on the inner planes. When the inner ashramic workers joined us, fully participating, we undertook the physical group formation work. The Initiate was a senior member of K.H.'s ashram, on the Second Ray, and a member of the Brotherhood of the Star.

The Brotherhood of the Star is known under many names and is the inner working body of the New Group of World Servers, the inner group of the New Group of World Servers one might say. It has no particular Ray affiliation and is simply a term to describe those, on the inner levels, who have chosen to work with the externalisation of the Hierarchical process. It is not a Ray ashram and should not be thought of as such. Therefore, masters and initiates are connected to it in one endeavour yet are still members of their particular Ray ashram, as much as members of the New Group of World Servers also belong to different Ray ashrams yet come together for one purpose.

Recently, I read of another term for the same group, but the description is exactly the same. Terms of reference are just that, a way of describing something and some may describe that same thing differently as in language, but it alters not the core of the thing referred.

Back in Krishnamurti's day of the Order of the Star, this was a conscious attempt to externalise this Brotherhood and create an early version of the New Group of World Servers as we now know it.

The Twelves Group's work was within this group and fully a part of it, just as there are other subsections of this worldwide group undertaking other work, some consciously, but most unconsciously. The Initiate came to represent two forces, that of the ashram of K.H. and, more specifically, that of the Brotherhood of the Star (as we knew it).

One of the tools received from The Initiate was an Invocation to be used supplementary to the Great Invocation given to the world by the Master DK in 1945. It was specifically laid out that this invocation was to be used in the Twelves work. In the preparation for the Twelves work, it was widely distributed, in several languages, through cards, bookmarks and posters. Contact with The Initiate was intense and requires great focus and reception. He told us, before we received it, that the invocation would take great focus from him and that it would represent a powerful tool for the group. This invocation would be one of the purest forms of the teaching regarding group work that The Initiate gave, which was transmitted, in sections, from July 1982 to Oct 1982. It was called "The Disciple's Invocation" (followed by three OMs):

THE DISCIPLE'S INVOCATION

May the Flame of the One find the
crucible of your being
May the Mighty One issue forth from on High
May Love Eternal and Love Inclusive Rule over All

Let the Flame spin upon the Way
Let the Light stand Revealed
Let the Seeker Become the Rose

May the tide of illusion be turned
May the Great Work be completed
May the White Ones issue Their Ultimatum

Let the Ultimatum be heard by those who
have ears to hear
Let them have insight and knowledge
that they may understand
Let them choose aright and with free will

And in so choosing let Peace come to Earth

This invocation was used by group members at our annual Gatherings and during members' personal meditations. We had set up a very active Triangles network of our members to train everyone in the techniques required and focus us all on cooperative effort. The network worked very well, although there were the occasional requests to change Triangles from participants for varying reasons.

A monthly newsletter was sent out to keep everyone in touch, and annual Gatherings were widely anticipated by all of us. We decided not to hold distant or virtual Twelves, as we were informed that keeping focus for Triangles was difficult enough for the vast majority, so executing a Twelve at a distance was fraught with problems such as lack of focus. We will develop this later.

The Initiate observed from afar and was often felt by members during meditation sessions or, on occasion, through their individual meditation practice at home. As time progressed, the ashram became an ever-real presence in our lives, with many members experiencing personal insights. As I occasionally spoke to members over the past years, post the group's work, often I have heard them say how the Twelves Group still affected them. For all of us, I think it fair to say, those days are remembered with deep love and affection. We do not know The Initiate's name, nor do we need to. In the early days, he signed himself K.H. as the whole ashram is embraced with K.H.'s energy. An initiate undertaking work often signs for the ashram and represents the Master of that ashram, as a stepping down process is always needed to enable the energy to be absorbed and distributed. Of course, the more rarefied and advanced the disciple, the closer to the actual source possible. In my life, this was not the case, as it was with Blavatsky, Bailey, or Roerich, who were advanced initiates themselves. Therefore, the channel was clearer and more focussed, as they had to receive huge amounts of information.

When undertaking work, the Hierarchy often just chose the best that was available or those who had incarnated for that specific purpose, interwoven with their disciples' own personal karma of course, as the two always had to synchronize.

It is open to debate as to whether The Initiate was the same individual throughout the twenty-year cycle. That is to say, was it always the same individual instructing all of the physical Twelves? I honestly don't know the full answer, but the ashramic energy was constant and, in fact, grew in potency over the years. What I am certain about is that the individual whom I term The Initiate delivered the 1982 collection of instructions which formed the foundations of the group work. This individual stepped down the energies and impressed my consciousness with the higher telepathy techniques, but, more importantly, he took part and guided the physical Twelves, often being felt in the room by participants, some of whom often saw lights etc. There was also the Devic presence at the pinnacle of the funnel created by the Twelve itself, which was the full focus of the work (more on this later).

With all hierarchical work, the energy withdraws and is dissipated, and this has happened to many groups over the years. The Twelves Group was an experiment, and, as such, the full potential of Twelves was never going to be fully realised. With our group, the energy was withdrawn, and I have had no contact or, at least, no conscious contact with The Initiate for over 20 years. In fact, it is fair to say, I have had no ashramic contact, or if I have unconsciously, this has been minor in comparison, over that active time.

To give a little perspective of time, the group began at the beginning of 1982, but the very first physical Twelve did not take place until Wesak Festival 1994, a full 12 years after the group's commencement. Why is that? The answer can be found in the slow, it seemed to us, unravelling of The Initiate's work with the group.

We have been told this was due to the varied nature of the group's members. Some were advanced initiates, some disciples, and some aspirants. On occasion, if we were having problems getting an actual Twelve organised, we took a person who was sympathetic but not actually on the pathway as yet, carrying them as best we could.

This was far from ideal and did lead to some problems of an energetic nature. The ideal, of course, would be twelve disciples, trained and focussed and, maybe, even with the same Ray makeup, but this was an impossible dream; we did what we could with what we had. Often, we would have 8/9 trained and very able disciples who would make up the 'core' 6 or 9 in the formation and they would anchor for everyone, including the 3 or 4 who were less advanced. This was quite hard work.

On the inner planes, I cannot give much comment. Did the inner ashram mirror the Twelve? What was the structure they used to channel the energy through us, apart from the funnel? We didn't have those answers, and all we could do was to be open to that work, secure in the knowledge that the Twelves had a Ring-PassNot, and, once the formation was established, naught that was not of Light could enter. However, it would be quite wrong to suggest we knew what the purpose, in its larger sense, was. Many groups work this way by opening themselves to serve where needed without knowing the detail. The only difference was degree. Our experiment was a little more focussed, with a specific magical number of participants that, in some way, unlocked a greater energy or, it might be better put, facilitated a greater energy from another source (i.e. the ashram). There is no question that group formation, in Triangles, Sixes, Nines and Twelves adds potency to the endeavour: the whole is much greater than the sum of all of the individuals.

We set out in our Twelve Guidelines manual the requirements for participants:

"Each light worker takes on the mantle of the Twelves Group by offering full attention and focus to the specific work of Twelves in a soul-conscious manner. Each light worker agrees to set aside the personality and other kinds of group work and activity throughout the time period of undertaking Twelves work. There is a commitment to be present from beginning to completion of the Work and to focus 100% on the Work in hand.

It is vital to the success of this particular spiritual energetic work that other tools and methods of light work are not allowed to filter into the process of the Star Gatherings. This will provide a 'quality assurance' for the energetic resonance of our Work.

We recognise that many Twelves Group light workers may be involved as members and/or leaders of other spiritual groups and activities. We do ask that when you work with the group as a Twelves Group worker you honour and respect the purity of this specific group work."

We were fortunate to have members who understood the significance of the experimental group work we were undertaking and were willing to suspend their other work whilst engaged in a Twelve. This is easier said than done, as most of our membership had deep involvement in other esoteric groups (Theosophical Society, Lucis Trust, Institute of Planetary Synthesis, University of the Seven Rays, Agni Yoga etc.).

None of the work we undertook, thankfully, challenged any of the core philosophies of any of the other groups; it was just a question of suspension whilst engaged and, in fact, our work complemented the other group work people were doing, as it pushed the boundaries of experience by actually doing. This is aptly demonstrated by Robert's group file note from September 1983:

"I feel we could now be beginning a new cycle of activity, up to now we have been laying the foundations and have achieved a steady outer work, contacts and inner orientation. The Preparatory Stage could now be complete especially as we both again feel the impulse for fresh research and a new longing to really clarify the work and know where we are placed. This has been building for some while and the content of the newsletter seven shows this development. We have also made interesting new contacts which would indicate an attractive pull.

We still have a small gap to bridge before Implementation can begin. That gap is in energy and once achieved will establish a magnetic center. We need a strong rhythm of 'Standing Forth' in the Light, centering within the Triangle Divine and using from this perspective the Disciples Invocation. We must become the Rose and reveal the Light of the Triad, transmuting the dross through the purificatory power of light/fire and during our meetings we should study all the pieces and pay particular attention to the Three Fires, Cosmic Twelves, Planetary Sevens and the Disciples invocation. This way we can prepare ourselves fully for the next stage of the work. Meditation on all the symbols given would also prove productive using the intuition and centering in the Head Center.

The keys to the work now unfolding have been given, this is now the time to really get off to work and know what we will be doing in groups etc. It implies the work of transmuting negative elements into cosmic positive force for good. Raising the mass emotional energy by casting the dross into the great fire and thus purifying and transmuting.

It can be argued that as this applies to action through the Will, Electric Fire and Kundalini we will be forming a connection to Shamballa and no doubt this will be achieved through structures of Twelve as we have been told. We are asked to become alchemists in the Great Work."

Robert, here in this personal note to me, sets the tone well and gives hints as to the work ahead. As I mentioned previously, Peter Maslin joined us as the third member of the core triangle, and Peter was an Alice Bailey expert of some standing. Peter saw the potential of Twelves, and his steadfastness to hold to the light had to be seen to be believed; most of us were in awe of him, it must be said.

Without these two fundamentally key individuals, the Twelves work was a non-starter. I just could not have done it, and I give them my eternal thanks for accompanying me on that pathway.

Both Robert and Peter passed away within a few years of each other, towards the end of the Twelves work. They were called home to the ashram for further expansive work as their work here, beside me, was completed. I pay tribute to them here.

Giants they were.

Shed no tears of sorrow for the transient nor bear grief for the departed for they are but an hour in the Glorious day."

The Initiate March 1982

Chapter Three

———◦———

The Significance of Twelve

FROM DISTANT TIMES, and in distant ways, up until modern times, practitioners of the sacred and magical arts have worked in groups within a circle of protection. A circle has no beginning or end; hence, practitioners cast a sacred circle to represent the macrocosm and the microcosm and produce the thought form that exists to protect those working within the circle.

It can be seen as a container, keeping within its ring-pass-not the working energy and blocking without energies and entities that are unwelcome. Our world consists of vibrating sounds, lights and colours and we measure time in cycles with clocks, calendars, zodiacal wheels etc.

A circle, then, has been used for millennia and has the power of certain numbers. For the purposes of undertaking magical and sacred work, combinations of people, in particular formations, the circle has greater protections and ability to work with forces of regeneration and energy than individuals alone or in haphazard numbers. Hence, three, six, nine and the definitive end number twelve have special potency for working with spiritual, sacred energies, and this has been the case since Plato and before.

Twelve is the number of completion. Numbers have always had mystical significance, and a whole science was based around these significances. People believe numbers linked with the alphabet, the stars, and the constellations. The number twelve represented the hours of day and night, the months of the year, and the zodiac. Sumerian priests first divided the year into twelve months of about thirty days each, and their day had twelve units so the number twelve became the unit of dividing time.

China had their twelve animals, Egypt her goddesses linked to the twelve hours of day and night. As above, so below, and the twelves represents the very creation of our universe and what we use in modern times to divide out time, vibrations, and tones.

As an example, the archeometre is an ancient template that forms from a twelve-pointed Star. Marquis Saint-Yves d'Alveydre, the French nineteenth-century magician, said the Archeometre was an instrument for predicting events and coordinating all human knowledge:

"The Archeometre is the instrument used by the Ancients for the formation of the esoteric myths of all religions. It is the canon of ancient Art in its various architectural, musical, poetic, and theogonic manifestations.

It is the Heaven that speaks: every star, every constellation becomes a letter or a phrase, or a divine name lighting the ancient traditions of all peoples with a new day."

Archeometre

Archeometre H. P. Blavatsky has stated that the visible universe, "was built on the model of the first DIVINE IDEA," which has always existed. HPB taught that, just as the soul of the universe is the Central Spiritual Sun, so also the sun is the soul which is built by the One, who constructed it "on the geometrical figure of the dodecahedron." HPB was referring to Plato who stated:

"The Universe was built by the "First-Born" on the geometrical figure of the Dodecahedron, a figure having twelve sides. This is typified in the twelve signs of the Zodiac."

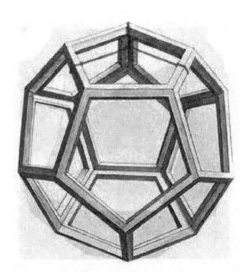

Dodecahedron

The great esotericist Manly P. Hall says this in regard to the number twelve:

"The number twelve frequently occurs among ancient peoples, who in nearly every case had a pantheon consisting of twelve demigods and goddesses presided over by The Invincible One, who was Himself subject to the Incomprehensible All-Father. This use of the number twelve is especially noted in the Jewish and Christian writings.

The twelve prophets, the twelve patriarchs, the twelve tribes, and the twelve Apostles--each group has a certain occult significance, for each refers to the Divine Duodecimo, or Twelvefold Deity, whose emanations are manifested in the tangible created Universe through twelve individualized channels…

…As these 12 (the three substances, salt, sulphur and mercury) existing in the four worlds, as shown in the table, sum up to the number 12. As these 12 are the foundations of The Great Work (alchemical), they are called in revelation the twelve foundation stones of the sacred city."

SECRET TEACHINGS OF THE AGES

In the 1920s, the magician Frater Achad experimented with 3-D projections of the Kabbalistic Tree of Life. He modelled the Tree as emanating from a single point in six directions and found the projections culminated in a dodecahedron.

Plutarch also wrote about this twelve of creation:

"The nature of the dodecahedron, which is comprehensive enough to include the other figures, may well seem to be a model with reference to all corporeal being."

In the Bible, the number 12 is mentioned 187 times, and the significance is huge as it represents the number for God.

In Revelations alone the number is mentioned 22 times, so the significance can be seen, clearly.

That this magical number represents the entire universe and the sacred going on therein–it is the number of completion, of wholeness, and of unity.

Jesus took 12 disciples who were to become the 12 Apostles. In Revelations, 144,000 would be saved, and the New City of Jerusalem had 12 gates attended by 12 Angels. The walls are 144 cubits high and 12,000 furlongs squared. Twelve precious crystals, or stones, would become the foundation of this New Jerusalem.

Here are some well-known examples from Revelation:

Revelation 12:1

"A great sign appeared in heaven: a woman clothed with the sun, and the moon under her feet, and on her head a crown of twelve stars;"

Revelation 21:12

"It had a great and high wall, with twelve gates, and at the gates twelve angels; and names were written on them, which are the names of the twelve tribes of the sons of Israel."

Revelation 21:14

"And the wall of the city had twelve foundation stones, and on them were the twelve names of the twelve apostles of the Lamb."

Revelation 22:2

"In the middle of its street on either side of the river was the tree of life, bearing twelve kinds of fruit, yielding its fruit every month; and the leaves of the tree were for the healing of the nations."

Although Revelations is the most oft quoted, there are other significant mentions of twelve:

Matthew 19:28

"And Jesus said to them, 'truly I say to you, that you who have followed Me in the regeneration when the Son of Man will sit on His glorious throne, you also shall sit upon twelve thrones.'"

Mark 3: 13-19

"And He went up on the mountain and summoned those whom He Himself wanted, and they came to Him. And He appointed twelve, so that they would be with Him and that He could send them out to preach."

Luke 6: 12-16

It was at this time that He went off to the mountain to pray, and He spent the whole night in prayer to God. And when day came, He called His disciples to Him and chose twelve of them, whom He also named as apostles."

John 11:9

"Jesus answered, 'Are there not twelve hours in the day? If anyone walks in the day, he does not stumble, because he sees the light of this world.'"

The Twelve Apostles in the New Testament were chosen by Jesus to be the government that he would leave behind to continue His work. Not just any old number, it was specific and ordained by God.

And so in the Christian tradition, it can clearly be seen the number twelve was crucial and was recognised as THE cosmic number.

But it wasn't only the Christians who recognised the sacredness of the number twelve: 12 masonic signs of recognition, 12 followers of the Buddha, 12 nights of the Round Tables, 12 followers of Quetzalcoatl, 12 Olympians, 12 labours of Hercules, 12 petals of the Anahata Chakra, and so on.

The Zoroastrians state:

"Twelve Signs of the Zodiac are the Twelve Commanders on the side of Light."

These commanders, according to Zoroastrians, fought against evil in the battle for the world's fate, whilst Buddhists state that life is composed of 12 stages, which, as a completion, keep the Wheel of Life turning. Within its grasp, life exists in Samsara until we find enlightenment and break free of the wheel.

The number twelve expanding upon itself to become 144 with twelve groups of Twelve working in harmony would lead to a tremendous unlocking of the forces of nature, we are told, and would lead to the ultimate in group work--the Twelve becoming the New Jerusalem and being the New Jerusalem here on earth (a portion of the New Jerusalem and facilitating its quickening).

The number twelve is the number of the people of God and the magical number that worked in complete harmony with nature, the earth, and the cosmos.

The Twelves Group was instructed to become a Bridge of Light between the ashram and those working for the externalisation of the Hierarchy on our earth. It was an early, basic experimental work with great potential for future group work. It sowed the seed, tilled the earth a little, and watered the seedling.

We cast the circle of protection, we enter the sacred space in right thought and mind and we assemble, firstly in threes, then sixes, then nines, and then ultimately in a

Twelve--reflecting our cosmos, God, nature, our very earth as we undertook this ritual 7th Ray training to Cast our Lot into the Chalice of Fire:

I am the Flame and the Rock I affirm!

I am the Light Divine and the Waters quench me not I affirm!

I am the center of my universe and I Stand I affirm!

And in standing thus I resolve to Serve Him

The Initiate, August 1986

Much of the work of Groups of Twelve was in the area of dispelling glamour and thought forms, creating cleavage within those thoughtforms so that entry points might be established for Hierarchy to undertake work (we did not know what this specific work was in detail).

We worked mostly with the cities of London, New York, and Moscow, and we held a Twelve in the first two of these but were unable to get us all to Moscow to physically hold a Twelve there. I did visit Moscow and linked in with the group from Red Square, but we found, over the years, that absent or virtual linkage had a slight connection but was very weak compared to the focussed intent of participants being physically in formation. The Master Djwhal Khul, through Alice Bailey, spoke much about the future work of groups in dispelling glamour:

"Their work will largely be to summarise and make effective the work of those two great Sons of God, the Buddha and the Christ. As you know, One of Them brought illumination to the world and embodied the principle of wisdom, and the Other brought love to the world and embodied in Himself a great cosmic principle—the principle of love. How can the effectiveness of Their work be brought about? The process will follow three lines:

1. Individual effort, made by the individual disciple, using the technique of detachment, of dispassion and of discrimination which the Buddha taught.

2. Group initiation made possible by the self-initiated effort of individual disciples, following out the injunctions of the Christ and leading to a complete subordination of the personality and of the unit to group interest and group good.

3. Group endeavour, carried forward as a group, to love all beings and to apprehend and the true significance of the Aquarian technique of group love and work."

Alice A. Bailey, *Discipleship in the New Age Volume 1*

I. The Technique of the Presence, when successfully followed, enables the intuition to flow in and to supersede the activity of the rationalising mind and to dispel illusion, substituting for that illusion divine ideas, formulated into concepts which we call ideals. The Masters, it should be remembered, only use the mind for two activities:

a. To reach the minds of Their disciples and attract aspirants through the medium of an instrument similar to the disciple's mind.

b. To create thought-forms on concrete levels which can embody these divine ideas. The directing Agent, the Angel of the Presence, produces the power to create in this manner, and this we call the result of the intuition—idea or truth, its perception and its reproduction.

II. The Technique of Light is more closely related to the mind and signifies the method whereby the illumination which flows from the soul (whose nature is light) can irradiate not only ideals but life, circumstances and events, revealing the cause and the meaning of the experience.

When the power of the disciple to illumine is grasped, he has taken the first step towards dispelling glamour; and just as the technique of the Presence becomes effective upon the mental plane, so this technique produces powers which can become effective on the astral plane and eventually bring about the dissipation and the disappearance of that plane.

III. The Technique of Indifference renders ineffective or neutralises the hold of substance over the life or spirit, functioning in the three worlds, for soul is the evidence of life.

It will be apparent to you, therefore, that groups working consciously at the service of dissipating glamour will have the following characteristics:

1. They will be composed of sixth ray aspirants and disciples, aided by second ray spiritual workers.

2. They will be formed of those who:

    a. Are learning or have learnt to dissipate their own individual glamour's and can bring under standing to the task.

    b. Are focussed upon the mental plane and have, therefore, some measure of mental illumination. They are mastering the Technique of Light.

    c. Are aware of the nature of the glamour's which they are attempting to dissipate and can use the illumined mind as a searchlight.

3. They will count among their numbers those who (occultly speaking) have the following powers in process of rapid development:

    a. The power not only to recognise glamour for what it is, but to discriminate between the various and many types of glamour. The power to appropriate the light, absorbing it into themselves and then consciously and scientifically project it into the world of glamour. The Masters, the higher initiates and the world disciples do this alone, if need be, and require not the protection of the group or the aid of the light of the group members.

b. The power to use the light not only through absorption and projection but also by a conscious use of the will, carrying energy upon the beam of projected light. To this they add a persistent and steady focus. This beam, thus projected, has a twofold use: It works expulsively and dynamically, much as a strong wind blows away or dissipates a dense fog or as the rays of the sun dry up and absorb the mist.

It acts also as a beam along which that which is new and a part of the divine intention can enter. The new ideas and the desired ideals can come in "on the beam," just as the beam directs and brings in the airplanes to a desired landing place."

Alice A. Bailey, *Glamour: A World Problem*

It is important to note here the sentence:

"They will be composed of sixth ray aspirants and disciples, aided by second ray spiritual workers."

We had a mix of Second and Sixth Rays in the Twelves Group (although the outer, ritual work was 7th Ray), and it brought with it its own problems that we attempted to work through over the years. The dedicated core of the group were all Second Ray disciples working with, mostly but not all, Sixth Ray participants. This inevitably led to problems of focus, especially in the early days, and ensured that the Work could only unwind slowly over many years.

As can be seen, the Twelves Group was a very early experiment utilising cosmic patterns and forces about which it was learning, slowly, by application. It cannot be overemphasised how difficult this was, as it had never been attempted before and was way ahead of its time. We only glimpsed at the possibilities, and, obviously, we had our own personal lives to attend to as well as this attempt at cosmic reflection. We made many mistakes, I made many mistakes, but the mistakes were never about the foundation of the Work, the cosmology, the linking with the ashram etc. They were always mistakes of the personality, time constraints, and the like, and I hope to go into those a little bit more later on.

A further good summary of the importance of the number Twelve is in J.E. Corlot's famous work *A Dictionary of Symbols:*

"Twelve Strictly, of all the numbers, twelve is the broadest in scope, for the Tarot formulas are such that they contain two groups of eleven and four of fourteen, but the components of these numbers have no archetypal significance. Given that the two essential prototypes of quantity are the numbers three and four (signifying respectively dynamism or inner spirituality, and stability or outer activity), it can be argued that their sum and their multiplication give the two numbers which are next in importance: seven and twelve. The latter corresponds to the geometrical dodecagon; but it may also be associated with the circle, since their symbolic meaning is practically identical. For this reason, systems or patterns based upon the circle or the cycle tend to have twelve as the end limit. Even when structures are made up of less than twelve elements at first, they later tend towards the superior number of twelve, as, for example, in music, where the seven-note modal scale has developed into the twelve-note system of the Arnold Schoenberg School.

Other examples are: the twelve hours on the clock-face; the twelve months of the year; the twelve major gods of many mythologies, as a kind of amplification of the seven planets; and the markings of the wind-rose (corresponding to Eurus, Solanus, Notus, Auster, Africus, Euroauster, Zephyrus, Stannus, Ireieus, Boreas, Aquilo, Volturnus). All these examples, then, prove the existence of an order founded upon patterns of twelve, which can be split up either into the 'inner' three-part division of the 'outer' or circumstantial pattern of four, or else into the 'outer' four-part division of the 'inner' and actual pattern of three. For the Vedic Indians, the twelve middle days of winter (from Christmas to Epiphany) were an image and a replica of the entire year; and a similar tradition exists in China. In our view, the symbolism of the Zodiac lies at the root of all these systems based upon the number twelve, that is, the idea that the four elements may appear in three different ways (levels or grades), giving twelve divisions. It is for these reasons that SaintYves draws the sociological conclusion that, among groups of human beings in the line of symbolic tradition, 'the circle which comes highest and nearest to the mysterious center, consists of twelve divisions representing the supreme initiation (the faculties, the virtues and knowledge) and corresponding, among other things, to the Zodiac'. Guenon (who quotes the above) adds that the twelve-formula is to be found in the 'circular council' of the Dalai Lama, and (quite apart from the twelve apostles) in the legendary Knights of the Round Table…"

And in another book of similar title:

"Twelve is the number by which space and time are divided, being the product of the FOUR points of the compass multiplied by the THREE levels of the universe. The vault of Heaven is divided into twelve sections, the twelve signs of the ZODIAC, to which reference has been made from the remotest past. In China, the twelve months of the year were determined by the stance of the emperor at the twelve gates of the Temple of Heaven. Among the Assyrians, Jews and other peoples, twelve split the year into twelve months and among the Chinese and the peoples of central Asia, into their principal periods of time, twelve-year cycles. Multiplying twelve by five provided a sixty-year cycle, at the end of which both solar and lunar cycles coincide. Twelve symbolizes the universe in its cyclical revolution in space and time.

It also symbolizes the inner complexity of the universe.

The group of twelve characteristics of the months of the year and the signs of the Zodiac may also stand for the multiplication of the four elements of Earth, Water, Fire and Air by the three alchemical principals of sulphur, salt and mercury; or else the three states of each element at the successive stages or their evolution, culmination and involution.

This number is especially rich in Christian symbolism: By multiplying the four of the world of space with the three of the sacred period of time measuring creation and recreation, we obtain twelve, which is the number of universal fulfilment which is that of the Heavenly Jerusalem with its twelve gates, of the twelve apostles and twelve foundations and so on, as well as being that of liturgical cycle of the year with its twelve months and their cosmic expression as the twelve signs of the Zodiac. In a more mystic sense, three relates to the Trinity and four to the creation, but the symbolism of twelve remains the same-a fulfilment of the earthly and created absorbed into the divine and uncreated.

It is easy to understand the importance of this number. To Biblical writers twelve was the number of the elect, that of God's Chosen People and of the Church, since Jacob (Israel) had twelve sons who became the ancestors of and gave their names to the twelve tribes of the Israelites (Genesis 35:23ff.). The Tree of Life bore twelve fruits and there were twelve jewels on the High Priest's breastplate. Thus, when Jesus chose twelve apostles, he openly announced his claim to choose, in God's name, another People (Matthew 10: 1ff.). The Heavenly Jerusalem has twelve gates on which are written the names of the twelve tribes of Israel and its walls have twelve foundations in the names of the twelve apostles (Revelations 21: 12, 14). The Woman clothed with the Sun (Revelations 12: 1) wore upon her head a crown with twelve stars. At the end of time, the number of the faithful will be 144,000, 12,000 from each of the twelve tribes of Israel (Revelations 7:4-8; 14:1).

Similarly, this City to come, 'in fine gold', rests upon twelve foundations each bearing the name of an apostle and forms a cube with sides 12,000 furlongs long and with walls of jasper 144 cubits high. This symbolic number, 12,000, is the product of one thousand (the symbol of a multitude) multiplied by the number of Israel itself (twelve), and it is that of the old and new Chosen People.

As for the number of the faithful, 144,000 is twelve squared multiplied by one thousand, and symbolizes the multitude of those who believe in Christ, the figure twelve standing for the Church, the Church triumphant after its successive phases of Church militant and persecuted Church.

Twelve may be defined as the number of fulfilment and of the completed cycle. Thus, in the Tarot, the twelfth major arcanum (the Hanging Man) marks the end of an involutionary cycle, the next card (XIII) being Death, which should be understood in the sense of rebirth."

Jean Chevalier and Alain Gheerbrant: *The Penguin Dictionary of Symbols*

I hope this chapter conveys the why's of a Twelve: the cosmic nature of it, the reflection of the universe/God call it what you will. The magical, sacred combining of dedicated disciples to a unified cause that reflects "as above, so below".

We were dreamers and activists and as we walked together, we learned, stumbled, fell and got up again. We never understood the inner workings of all the whys and how's we just sought to serve – and we did.

Modern scientists are also recognising the significance of Plato's dodecahedron and the universal impact of the number twelve:

"An analysis of astronomical data suggests not only that the universe is finite, but also that it has a specific, rather rigid topology (dodecahedral sphere). If confirmed, this is a major discovery about the nature of the universe."

George F. R. Ellis, *"The Shape of the Universe",* Nature Magazine, Vol 425, October 9, 2003

This gives us sure hope that as modern science unfolds the Ancient Wisdom will be further ratified and it will be fully realised that, as in the Cosmo, so upon our earth and the key to regeneration and transmutation is a connection to both: the twelve to the twelve.

To end this part of our discussion the Twelves Group claims no originality as the concept of twelve as a magical number. As can be seen it goes back to the Apostles, Plato and all the rest.

We claim only APPLICATION of known principals and attendance to group experiment.

"Here is your field of service: The World

Here is your surety of success: The Hierarchy

Here is your home: The Soul"

The Initiate Jan 1983

Chapter Four

The Group in Action

BEFORE WE PROCEED upon our journey and describe the Twelve Groups work through those years, it is imperative that we mention, yet again, the experimental nature of the thing.

Probably the best way is to quote DK in the book *Esoteric Psychology 2* where he lays it out very succinctly and, although the quotation is more lengthy than I would like to include in this book (remembering my promise concerning book quotations) it is such an important piece as far as the Twelves Group is concerned, and of course future group work, that it really is worth noting here:

"I have said that these groups constitute an experiment. This experiment is fourfold in nature and a concise statement about it may clarify conjecture:

I.   They are an experiment in founding or starting focal points in the human family through which certain energies can flow out into the entire race of men. These energies are ten in number.

II. They are an experiment in inaugurating certain new techniques in work and in modes of communication... It is to be noted that in these last three words is summed up the whole story. These groups are intended to facilitate interrelation or communication as follows:

1. They will be occupied with an endeavour to facilitate communication between individuals so that the rules and methods whereby speech can be transcended may become known and the new way of intercourse be brought about. Eventually communication will be from:

    a. Soul to soul, on the higher levels of the mental plane. This involves complete alignment, so that soul-mind-brain are completely at-one.

    b. Mind to mind, on the lower levels of the mental plane. This involves the complete integration of the personality or lower self, so that mind and brain are at-one.

    c. Students must remember these two distinctive contacts, and bear in mind also that the greater contact need not necessarily include the lesser. Telepathic communication between the different aspects of the human being is entirely possible at varying stages of unfoldment.

2. They will work at the establishment of communication between that plane which is the plane of illumination and pure reason (the buddhic plane) and the plane of illusion which is the astral plane. It should be remembered that our great task is to dispel the world illusion through the pouring in of illumination or of light.

When enough groups have been started that have this for their objective, there will then be found upon the physical plane, those channels of communication which will act as the mediators between the world of light and the world of illusion.

3. Through other groups another type of energy must flow, producing another type of interrelation and communication. These groups will bring about the right healing of the personalities of individuals, in all aspects of their nature. The work intended is the intelligent transmission of energy to various parts of the nature—mental, astral and physical— of the human being, through the right circulation and organisation of force. Healing must eventually be carried forward by groups which act as the intermediaries between the plane of spiritual energy (either soul energy, intuitional energy, or will energy) and the patient or group of patients. This last point is to be noted. The group idea must always be remembered, for this will distinguish the New Age methods from the past; the work will be group work for the group. The members will work as souls and not as individuals. They will learn to communicate healing energy from the reservoir of living force to the patients.

4. Other groups of communicators will act as transmitters of two aspects of divine energy, —

knowledge and wisdom. These must be thought of in terms of energy. Their work will concern itself with the education of the masses, as a direct intermediary between the higher mind and the lower mind, and with the building of the antaskarana; and their task is that of linking the three points of interest upon the mental plane,— the higher mind, the soul, and the lower mind— so that there is established a group antaskarana between the kingdom of souls and the world of men.

5. Political work will occupy other groups more specifically than does any other branch of work. These groups communicate the "quality of imposition" and an authority that is lacking in many other branches of this divine group activity. The work is largely first ray work. It embodies the method whereby the divine Will works out in the consciousness of races and nations. Members of this group will have much first ray in their constitution. Their work is to act as channels of communication between the department of the Manu and the race of men. It is a noble thing to be channels of the Will of God. Some groups will be, in a pronounced sense, channels between the activity of the second ray, that of the World Teacher (at the present time, the Christ holds this office) and the world of men.

The energy of the second ray must pour through such groups of students and believers and allied groups of thinkers and workers, and there will be many of these. This fact is to be noted. There will be many such groups. The platform of the new world religion will be built by them.

A few groups will have an interesting function, but one which will not materialise for a long while, or not until the work of the building forces of the Universe are better understood. This will be coincident with the development of etheric vision. These groups will act as channels of communication or intermediaries between the energies which constitute the forces which construct the forms, the fabricators of the outer garment of God, and human spirits.

The possibility is, therefore, to be noted that the main initial work will be concerned with the problem of reincarnation. That problem deals with the taking of an outer garment or form under the Law of Rebirth. Therefore, when these groups are organised, it will be with that subject that the members will at first work. They will make a deeper and different study than has heretofore been undertaken on the Law of Rebirth.

Some groups of energy communicators and transmitters will carry illumination between groups of thinkers. They are illuminators of group thoughts. They transmit energy from one thought center to another. They transmit, above everything else, the energy of ideas. That is their major function. The world of ideas is a world of dynamic force centers. This should not be forgotten. These ideas have to be contacted and noted. Their energy has to be assimilated and transmitted and this is the function of those force centers which will express themselves along these lines of activity.

6. Groups working in another category will have for their specific work the stimulating of the minds of men so that alignment can take place. They act primarily as channels of communication between the soul of man and the soul in any form. They will be the great psychometrical workers, for a psychometrist is one whose soul is sensitive to the soul in other forms of life, —human and non-human. They evoke the soul of the past, primarily, linking it with t the present, and finding it also indicative of the future.

7. Members of other groups will be communicators between the third aspect of Deity as it expresses itself through the creative process and the world of human thought. They will link or blend life and form creatively. Today, unknowingly and without any true understanding, they bring about a concretisation of the energy of desire, which, in its turn, brings about the concretisation of money.

III. This, consequently, necessitates the materialisation of things. They have a most difficult task and that is why it is only during the past one hundred and fifty years that the science of world finance has made its appearance. They will deal with the divine aspect of money. They will regard money as the means whereby divine purpose can be carried forward. They will handle money as the agency through which the building forces of the universe can carry forward the work needed; and (herein lies the clue) those building forces will be increasingly occupied with the building of the subjective Temple of the Lord rather than with the materialising of that which meets mans desire. This distinction merits consideration. They are the externalisation of an inner existing condition. It must be realised that these Groups are not a cause but an effect. That they may themselves have an initiatory effect as they work upon the physical plane is no doubt true, but they themselves are the product of inner activity and of subjective aggregations of force which must perforce become objective. The work of the group members is to keep, as a group, in close rapport with the inner groups, which form nevertheless, one large, active group. This central group force will then pour through the groups in so far as the group members, as a group—

a. Keep *en rapport* with the inner sources of power;

b. Never lose sight of the group objective, whatever that objective may be;

c. Cultivate a dual capacity to apply the laws of the soul to the individual life, and the laws of the group to the group life;

d. Use all forces which may flow into the group in service, and learn, therefore, to register that force and use it correctly.

Would the following sequence of statements convey anything to our minds in this connection? It is a statement of fact and is not in the least symbolic in its terminology, except in so far as all words are inadequate symbols of inner truths.

1. Each group has its inner counterpart.

2. This inner counterpart is a complete whole. The outer result is only partial.

3. These inner groups, forming one group, are each of them expressive of, or governed by certain laws, embodying, the controlling factors in group work.

   A law is only an expression or manifestation of force, applied under the power of thought by a thinker or group of thinkers.

4. These inner groups, embodying differing types of force, and working synthetically to express certain laws are an effort to bring in new and

different conditions, and hence produce a new civilisation. This is the New Age that the Aquarian Age will see consummated.

5. The outer groups are a tentative and experimental effort to see how far humanity is ready for such an endeavour.

IV. They are also an experiment which has for its objective the manifestation of certain types of energy which will produce cohesion, or an atonement, upon earth. The present distraught condition in the world, the international impasse, the religious dissatisfaction, the economic and social upheaval of the past few decades, are all the result of energies that are so potent owing to their immense momentum— that they can only be brought into rhythmic activity by the imposition of stronger and more definitely directed energies. When the groups are functioning adequately and have achieved, not only an internal group unity, but also harmony between the groups themselves, then some peculiar and esoteric work can be done.

Such are some of the plans which the Hierarchy are attempting to carry forward and in which all true disciples and aspirants can have a part. They are brought to our attention in order to evoke our lasting cooperation."

Alice A. Bailey, *Esoteric Psychology 2*   DK instructions from

As stated beautifully by DK, group work, for the foreseeable future, is experimental and must be viewed as such. It is certainly not a question of, "Did we succeed, or did we fail?" but more of, "What did we do, how did we do it and what is to be learned?".

Star Gatherings were held at least annually, as described, with the first Twelve formation held in 1994. However, there were Gatherings annually from the early 1980s where we meditated, prepared and worked as a group to understand the purpose of us coming together and, of course, to further study The Initiate's instructions. I have selected, as examples, three of these Gatherings to give you a flavour of the endeavour.

NEW YORK 1987

We were honoured to be invited by our American members to present the group's work in New York, USA. Around half a dozen of us travelled from the UK and other members from Europe. We had a total of around 40/50 people attending (I can't quite remember exactly but enough to split into three large groups for discussion and reflection on three differing aspects of the group's future work ahead). There was a certain pressure, naturally, from participants to try a Twelve formation but it was felt the group was just not ready (and The Initiate indicated such) so we spent the week in New York holding the three group sessions (see picture of one of those groups) to discuss the work in progress and to integrate the group consciousness.

At the end of that week we gathered together for meditation practice and to share with each other insights we had gained during the process. This was frustrating for some participants who wanted to get on with it and we lost a few members by the wayside. Mostly, though, participants were patient and we had the group, ashramic meditations to focus on and so our time was well spent.

Peter leading one of the three discussion groups New York 1987

Robert Adams, Peter Maslin and myself, New York 1987

As I recall, Robert presented the group's purpose and intention, Peter presented DK's work of groups coupled with the Cosmic Alignment and I led the ashramic meditations and chipped in a bit here and there.

GLASTONBURY AND LONDON 1994

Our very first Twelve was held in Glastonbury and was so successful participants requested another, supplementary, meeting in London the same year. Regretfully, I do not have any photos of that first Twelve in 1994, only the London meeting that followed.

London 1994

We had prepared for our first Twelve over many years (twelve years in fact but this was not significant I believe, just coincidence?). The original format as given by The

Initiate changed little as time went on but the energies increased until around the late 1990s. The energies and ashramic connections eventual dissipated after the last Star Gathering in 1999 and the groups, final, closure came in 2002 exactly twenty years after it was founded.

Everyone in Glastonbury was very excited for this first Gathering that would include a Twelve formation as we had announced it would take place. When we arrived, we had all realised prior via the advance schedule that this was the year when we would actually attempt the group formation that we had discussed and meditated upon for so long.

We knew what we had to do and we selected the twelve participants for the first Twelve with others in the supporting role; they would have their chance to participate in the next day's Twelve, as we would hold two, so that everyone could take part.

The first two days was the usual ashramic group meditations and preparation for the day's first Twelve. This included mapping out the room with the Cardinal points of the compass represented by coloured pieces of paper and a candle at each point. This takes some time to get right as the twelve-pointed star is measured accurately and the positions where the participants would stand for the formation had to be exact.

Peter, with his scientific training, normally undertook this pedantic task, as we quickly learnt, that too many esotericists spoiled the star most of us, wisely, withdrew and let Peter do his thing (for which he was very grateful).

Peter (kneeling) preparing the sacred space 1994

The points were mapped out exactly and a candle placed at each point.

Firstly, we undertook the group meditation and split into the four triangles in separate parts of the room where OMs and group synthesis were practiced in readiness.

Tentatively, the first Triangle took position (the full format of the methodology of Twelves is detailed in Chapter 6) and connection was made. There was a real energy in the room and everyone was very much focussed on the task in hand. Secondly, the six was formed and then the nine and, lastly, the Twelve.

The ritual was undertaken, and a powerful force connected with the room and down the cone creating a vortex of light. Several participants were visibly shaken as we had to Hold the Light steady for a while on a few occasions.

As participants had their eyes closed, the reader might reasonably wonder, "How did we know that some were more affected?"

The group had decided, as mentioned earlier, that if there were enough participants the Focaliser would stand on the outside of the formation and guide and instruct the group. The reason for this was due to the energies being so strong that it takes infinitely more focus and drive to do so from within the Twelve (and I know as I have experienced both).

So, we completed our very first Twelve, and as far as we know, the first ever. We undertook a second Twelve the next day. It is fair to say the participants were exhausted. It took refinement of practice over the years to let it flow. Anyone that ever takes part in a Twelve is deeply affected by it on many levels. It IS a work and service that should not be underestimated.

We learnt over the years to prepare many weeks before a Twelve was to be undertaken. Mentally, physically and spiritually we had to be in shape. There were very rare occasions when we had to shut a Twelve because a participant was feeling overwhelmed, so we developed a protocol for this. * This is another reason why directing the Twelve's orchestra from the outside was far preferable than inside.

*Basically, the Focaliser would sound an OM and ask the group to slowly, and carefully withdraw the ray of light within their triangle into their heart center. This would be done sequentially, step by step, starting with triangle four. This took approximately 30 minutes, sometimes more. This was, in some ways a fractious process, and was to be avoided if at all possible. To build up the energy, get the protection in place then bring it down again was the last resort in an emergency (someone feeling faint, for example).

Glastonbury 1998

The Penultimate Gathering of 1998 (the photos are used in Chapter 6 as we don't have photos from 1999) was a tour de force on many levels.

As Robert and Peter had left us, I think many of us knew that this phase of the experiment was shifting in that we had set certain etheric, astral and mental thoughtforms and structures which would be utilised and learned from in the future.

It was nearly time to say goodbye and the Gathering in 1999 would be the last although during the Gathering I don't think anyone expected, apart from me, that this would be the last.

Glastonbury 1998

We had come together, we had loved and worked together, and we had grown together. Chapter 5 is a conglomeration of questions which might further add insight as to why the dissipation came. Esoteric work is not easy work as it deals with energies and time commitments whilst we all have other lives. We didn't have the luxury of simply dedicating ourselves to Twelves. People had families, careers and other activities.

While it is romantic to think of the disciple trudging the way, backpack and all, most of us live in the modern world and have responsibilities. I, for one, will hold my hand up and say, *Mea Culpa*, as I was, on occasion, too preoccupied with my career and passing my degrees so I let slip the focus on occasion (although at each Gathering I was very much present). Also, the loss of my beloved friends and co-workers Robert and Peter was difficult to put aside as they were integral to the Twelves Group and at the very heart of it. When the energy was withdrawn, they were needed elsewhere in the ashram. The experiment had completed Phase One.

I was present with Robert when he passed, lying on the bed in front of me and his parents. It was a blessed release for him and as I recited the Great Invocation over his dying breath, I remembered our times working together and I wished him bon voyage.

Peter's passing, although I knew he was seriously ill and had several telephone discussions with him, I learnt of from another Twelves Group member as everyone thought I would know. I knew he was gravely ill and had spoken to him on the telephone only a few days earlier, but it was a bit of a shock that he had suddenly gone.

I understand that at least one Twelves Group member was at the funeral but his parents, I understand, were hostile regarding his esoteric work. His soul was pulled back to the ashram and I knew that his work with us was finished, that he had other work to do. I also knew that the group needed to transmute and that the ashramic energy had dimmed. It takes courage to say, "Fare thee well".

Some members were resentful, and some hurt at the dissolution. It is an illusion as the work lives on, the experiment served its purpose and then the waiting... waiting for the time to come again when others shall raise the standard high and higher.

In the next Stage of Twelves, recently launched, some of those faithful coworkers have re-joined us as we once again take up the mantle of this work.

We also have many new coworkers and we are very fortunate to have many very experienced disciples from various parts of the esoteric genre each bringing a treasure trove of valuable insight.

Restarting?

*"These ancient tenets must be restored and lived;
retreats must be manifested."*

The Initiate Feb 1982

Chapter Five

―――――――●○◗―――――――

Questions from Friends, Enquirers and Coworkers

Would you say the experiment was a success?

It depends how we determine success. Is humanity a success? In the esoteric sphere success is very difficult to define as many things happen that we do not perceive, hidden energies, setbacks and achievements. Who is to say what is successful and what is not? The Twelves Group was taking part in an experiment. Not just an outer group experiment but an inner plane experiment to determine parameters for the future.

If we concentrate, just for a minute on the outer plane work, yes, we achieved limited success, within the timeframe, but not total success in my opinion. We were just a group of disciples and aspirants seeking to serve and test the limits (if there are any) of group synthesis whilst engaging with ashramic/hierarchal forces hitherto we had not known. These forces impact the group and the individual.

My individual reflection is that the experiment was partially successful but when it was realised that only limited success could be achieved the energy was withdrawn from the group and two of the core three triangle members withdrew their individual forces and moved on to inner plane working. It is obvious that these two great workers are now assisting the new group manifestation now called simply Twelves.

I would think preparing this account of the Twelves Group was at least one of those reasons as it was a work unfinished. I was unprepared to attempt it earlier (and the timing was not right) and, maybe, a little tardy but it is important to get this out there prior to the Major Hierarchal Impact in 2025. This coming date has tremendous significance for humanity and the externalisation: "This period started in the year 1825 and will continue until the end of this century. The unfoldment of the Christ life—as a result of the presence and activities of the second divine aspect of love—will result in the ending of economic fear, and the "house of bread" will become the "house of plenty." Bread—as the symbol of material human need—will eventually be controlled by a vast group of initiates of the first initiation—by those whose lives are beginning to be controlled by the Christ consciousness, which is the consciousness of responsibility and service.

These initiates exist in their thousands today; they will be present in their millions by the time the year 2025 arrives.

All this reorientation and unfoldment will be the result of the activity of the seventh ray and of the impact of its radiation upon humanity."

Alice A. Bailey, *The Rays and The Initiations*

I have expanded this theme considerably in Chapters 10, 11 and 12

Did the experience change you?

Not one of the participants was unaffected. It was impossible not to be affected when actively engaged with ashramic forces. It is disturbing too. Each of us was protected, not only by the Devic Presence and the protective circle around the group formation, but through our ability to interact with the ashramic forces.

Some were more advanced than others and it was always understood that we, as individuals, could only serve to our capacity and, ongoing that was one of the problems we encountered: how to get, and maintain, twelve disciplined and focussed disciples who were committed to working virtually between gatherings and prepared to travel and be physically present.

As explained earlier this was not a virtual group we need to be there physically and that put a strain on participants and the group as a whole. We were all changed and to this day feel that impact.

I have lost touch with most of the group but did get a chance to chat with many in the closing days and for a few years afterwards. The response was always the same, "Ah Twelves! That experience is etched into my soul" and "Momentous and I often remember the power, love and the healing, etc."

Those were typical comments. Strangely, though, we all felt the need to go our separate ways. It was almost, "Why be together" if not working? We came together, we served together, and we parted as comrades in the work to live out our remaining lives. But we would never forget.

Now, of course, several of those 'originals' are back working with the new Twelves alongside many wonderful new souls who have taken up the challenge.

Was it worth doing?

A disciple's effort, sincerely undertaken is never wasted. We cannot hope to see all the ramifications of our work. Like the alarm clock that is set, left unattended then goes off unexpectedly, what we do today, and what we did yesterday, will affect our futures. On a higher turn of the spiral it is the same with esoteric work.

We lay foundations for future work to be undertaken. Group work is not easy. Most esotericists I know are strident individuals, all working for Hierarchy in some capacity or another, but to then come into a group work is difficult for all of us. In my case I work much better as an individual than as part of a group, but it is in group work that the externalisation depends. Not brilliant individuals working alone, although great work can be achieved this way too, but group work is the future and through group synthesis and empowerment will change come. The Hierarchy is, after all, a group. The whole is greater than the sum of its parts thus building the vortex of light in strict group formation adds all those individuals' powers together then ramps that up 12-fold, then adds the inner groups power (ashram) increasing it to 144 exponentially.

Why write this book?

The Twelves Group ran, in one form or another, for 20 years and at the dissipation we all went our separate ways, but the experience of the experiment had to be consolidated and documented for that phase to be truly over. As we approach 2025 and the Great Convocation of Hierarchy it is important to get on record the group's experience:

"Thus, a great and new movement is proceeding, and a tremendously increased interplay and interaction is taking place. This will go on until A.D. 2025. During the years intervening between now and then very great changes will be seen taking place, and at the great General Assembly of the Hierarchy—held as usual every century—in 2025 the date in all probability will be set for the first stage of the externalisation of the Hierarchy. The present cycle (from now until that date) is called technically "The Stage of the Forerunner". It is preparatory in nature, testing in its methods, and intended to be revelatory in its techniques and results. You can see therefore that Chohans, Masters, initiates, world disciples, disciples and aspirants affiliated with the Hierarchy are all at this time passing through a cycle of great activity."

Alice A. Bailey, *The Externalisation of the Hierarchy*

It is quite possible that a group, in the future, will come to pick up this work of 'Twelves'. Much has been ingrained on the etheric, astral and mental by our group but it is also important to solidify, as best I can, the group endeavour in the hope that it might be useful to others at some future stage. Many of us hope for a major event in 2025, perhaps the reappearance of Maitreya, *in homine*, or a great outpouring of Love Wisdom the effects of which could spark, over hundreds of years, the externalisation. A renewed effort by some original and many new coworkers are rebooting Twelves and the expansion of the triangles network.

Would you change anything?

I am not a great believer in the phase, "no regrets" as I think none of us are perfect as we all make mistakes and misjudgements. For anyone to say, "I would change nothing" sounds arrogant to me. When I reflect on my life there are many things I would improve, things I would not say and kindnesses I would render more unequivocally.

In my group work the same applies. I took Robert and Peter for granted and wish I had not. I was very much absorbed in my studies and career and wish I was less so. I was ambitious and ruthless, on occasion, and wish it were not so.

We all develop and grow and as the Dalai Lama says:

"Time passes unhindered. When we make mistakes, we cannot turn the clock back and try again. All we can do is use the present well".

Would I change the actual Twelves?

No, I think we rarefied and improved the process over many years and achieved just about as much as we could have with the tools we had. If we could have proceeded there was the future work of 'Ray Twelves' (working with one of the Major Rays through the formation of Twelves--a work we never attempted nor were prepared for). Also, the work of multiple Twelves leading to the 12 x 12 one hundred and forty-four formation which, we were informed, might have group initiatory potential. Again, we were way in advance of our time and work with Rays or in 144 formation were way beyond our reach, but we knew of the potential, and this potential I share here.

Who was the Chinaman?

A couple of people have asked me this question and the truth is I don't know. I can only relate the fact that he arrived at Robert's house (where we ran the group) and told us that he had come from the ashram. Robert asked him how he found the address (as we used a postal box number). He said he had seen a star over the house and just followed it.

I cannot say to you I am 100% sure of who he was as I simply don't know. I relate the true story and leave you to ponder upon it. In my younger days I might have wistfully claimed this and that, but I resist these days and prefer to err on the side of caution. He came, an emissary he claimed, and he didn't say much but looked upon us knowingly, stayed about an hour and was on his way never to be seen again leaving an energy imprint that survives until this day.

Where are the members today?

As described earlier, the group's energy dissipated and was withdrawn. The fellowship and service ethic of the group had been so strong that it was rather an anti-climax when we wound down. I know of a few members that are also on my Blavatsky, Bailey, Roerich (BBR) group on Facebook, but most have gone their own ways and are no doubt working in some capacity with other groups.

Will you re-start the Twelves Group?

As it says in Ecclesiastes there is "a time to plant, and a time to pluck up what is planted" and the Twelves Group will not be restarted in the format it once was. I think it highly likely that another group, almost certainly under a different name, will take up the reigns again but who knows when as it depends on ashramic support. For real work connected to the externalisation it has to be sponsored by the Hierarchy and receive that ashramic support and energy. Will this happen before 2025 or 2125? I don't know and my task, now, is to close this chapter in my life and detail for others the events as they happened.

I am quite certain that groups of disciples will work in Twelve formation at some stage in the future for twelve is THE cosmic number that represents the heavens, reflects the divine and the New Jerusalem. It is the number of magic and transcendence. If a group were formed who wanted to explore this work I would gladly advise, and participate, but it is just as likely that this will not happen in my lifetime, but you never know...

not starting?

Do you have any ashramic contact or contact with The Initiate these days?

I had no contact with The Initiate nor with the ashram for many years although the link was always there. At the dissipation I lost all contact and only recently has it somewhat been restored. This was a shock at the time but time has taught that it was entirely natural as I thought my role was over. During those years I had undertaken a function, a role, and once that particular work was finished there was no need for contact. It must be stressed that real ashramic/Hierarchical contact is only ever made for a PURPOSE which is far beyond the individual's incarnation of personal karma. Withdrawing that contact is in no way any form of punishment; it is simply a withdrawal of focus much as anyone who drives a car then steps out after the journey in anyway does that in retribution. The car's job is simply completed.

I do not seek, nor do I ponder upon that contact. I accept it and move on. I hope, and trust, that I will have the opportunity to serve again and I will do so without emotion in service to the One. As of now (July 2019) we are rebuilding and expanding that original work.

Have you ever had any physical contact with the ashram?

Speculation regarding Chinamen aside there was no physical contact with the ashram. There was one incidence of help that was physical. It involved a manifestation of a bookmark with information upon it that answered a question that Robert and I had been, frankly, stressing over for some time. I shall recount it here for completeness:

I had received information, during a deep meditation via higher telepathy that a Master was working in the City of London through a certain building. This building was on a ley-line of great power and was being utilised as part of this Master's work. I received an impression which building that was and was asked to go there at a certain date and time. I was a little unsure and, I admit, I doubted the veracity of the information as it had not come via The Initiate whose energy I had worked with for so long and I knew his signature. I was connecting with the inner ashram and the information came to go to the building. I met with Robert, we discussed this and agreed that we would go as asked but I ruminated and shared my concern with Robert that although I was 100% sure the fact that it was an ashramic source I could not determine if the building I was shown was the actual building that we should visit.

We happened to be standing in my house at the time, near to the bookshelf, where I intuitively picked up the book *How A World Teacher Comes* by Annie Besant.

Out fell an old bookmark from the early 1900s with a picture of the very building on it. Confirmation.

The bookmark

We had been given an Invocation that was specific for London and asked to attend this place so off we went. We managed to get inside the building, we undertook a meditation with ashramic link-up then recited the London Invocation. I would like to report that we met the London Master but we did not, alas, though we were told that he was physically there. But apart from going up to hundreds of people asking them, "Are you the London Master"? It was futile--unless he presented himself (which he would only do so for a specific purpose not just to assuage our curiosity) then we had undertaken our task.

What about physical group work versus virtual?

There was an amazing leap forward after DK undertook his work with Alice Bailey and Lucis Trust was formed. The work of Triangles, started in 1937, has had a major beneficial impact on the world and been a conduit for the Hierarchy.

My contention is that this work was always planned to be expanded into sixes, nines and twelves. It is an extension, not a replacement, of that network. A hint of that is in the Triangles logo even now used by the Lucis Trust (a twelve-pointed star within another and within a third).

This work is absent or virtual. Lucis Trust does not encourage linkage between students who study with them. My opinion is that this loss of fellowship harms the work instead of enhancing it. Having said that, I deeply respect the work they have done and continue to do. This network is 1000s strong and people may join more than one triangle if they wish to do so. It not only is a phenomenal work in itself, as it pours the energy of Goodwill into the planet's etheric body and uses the Great Invocation daily, it also acts in a preparatory way for more powerful and focussed work in the future.

The work of Twelves was totally in person. We used triangles daily in a very similar way and only added a link to the Twelves Group as a focus in preparation for the group work. Twelves could not be undertaken virtually as it had a specific ritual-based focus. It would be like an orchestra playing a symphony without being able to see the conductor nor hear the other players. It might produce some noise, and some sort of tune, but not quite what the composer had it mind. We have now developed Distant Twelves and have overcome some of those issues – it seems that this second stage, Implementation, has added distant, virtual work to the obvious advantages of physical work that we developed earlier.

What do you see as the future of group work?

The work of the New Group of World Servers (NGWS) has been described in detail in the works of Alice Bailey with the Master Djwhal Khul and needs no expansion here. DK states:

"...working disciples everywhere when they meet each other, will know at once that their work is identical, and will advise with each other as to where cooperation and supplementary endeavour may be possible"

Alice A. Bailey, *A Treatise on White Magic*

I believe that group work will develop in a more conscious, physical formation and include useful work in Threes, Sixes and Nines and Twelves is the ultimate, logical, natural template.

What was to be the future work of Twelves?

There were three distinct potentials;

One intention was for the work to develop along the lines of the Rays. There would be three types of Twelves: First Ray, Second Ray and Third Ray. We do not know much about what that would entail in the field but we know it involved the work of thoughtform destruction, clearing of energy lines, building of lighted thoughtforms, healing and lastly creating energetic space for other work to be undertaken.

Secondly, as to participants, there was a clear intention to develop disciples to work within the group in a more focussed way and, eventually, according to Ray type. This would include a Twelve made up of those on the Second Ray (for example) thus giving clarity and focus for that particular work.

Thirdly, multiples of Twelves would add force and power in the same way as individuals do in group formation. Starting with Three Twelves, Six, Nine then progressing to Twelve. This last multiple aggregating into 144 which, we were told, would be the ultimate Force-for-Good. We can only speculate the marvellous and wonderful things that would occur.

It must be remembered that the science of Twelves is not new it has just been hidden through the years. In ancient Lemuria and Atlantis much work in group formation was undertaken and I think it highly likely that work in Groups of Twelve would have been known about and practiced as a key, or gateway, to universal energies.

The Initiate often talked about sleepers who, if the Note be well struck, would awaken to the group work.

Why did the Twelves Group dissipate?

Much as the Hierarchy withdrew Their energy from Krishnamurti (leading many to speculate that it was Krishnamurti who withdrew from the work when, in fact, it was the other way round – please see the Addendum), they also withdrew Their energy from the Theosophical Society and may have done the same with other organisations well known today, it was the same process.

It has to be emphasized that Masters only engage with disciples or aspirants for specific purposes then when that is achieved, they often withdraw, and the energy dissipates. Probably no organisation that has received Hierarchal sponsorship retains that longer term. The Twelves Group was leading edge, achieved the formation of the basic foundations for future group work in Twelves, and when that was accomplished and it was observed that the group could not further that clarion call any more than it already had Robert, then Peter, were withdrawn to other work within the ashram and the withdrawal of ashramic energy *they're back!*

proceeded over a couple of years and the group ceased to be in that from, it has now resurrected and strengthened. This is no guarantee of success, of course, but the times are urgent.

Were there any side effects of Twelves work?

Yes, working with the group had its usual tensions, sometimes personality led and other times just with practical issues. However, the biggest impact, or side effect was in the lives of participants. Many of us found it difficult just to return to our normal lives after a formation. Therefore the slow grounding following a Gathering was essential.

Many of us felt that our lives were pretty meaningless after the Work in the early days. Later we all learnt the Art of Balance and got better at placing the Twelves work in one box and our daily lives in another. There were some strained relationships with significant others who were not in attendance and, perhaps, had no interest in the group's work. It was an issue in my marriage and I am now divorced (in the 1980s) never to marry again. The life of an Esoteric Apprentice is a life alone although there are rare instances where this is not the case. I just find it easier and continue the work today.

Did you run into obstacles other than people?

Most Theosophical/Esoteric organisations become, after the first flush of youth and after the dissipation I talked about previously, stale and defensive of their way. This is a hindrance to all new initiatives. We have the traditional

Theosophists who cannot abide the Bailey adherents and we have the Agni Yoga organisation at loggerheads with Lucis Trust so these three branches are in disunity.

Thank goodness most esotericists I know reject all of that noise and love and respect all three. However, each has fallen into the same trap themselves and only support those organisations that adhere to their values and teachings.

The Twelves Group was made up of members from each of these three branches but if the original organisations were more open then, obviously, a great cooperation would ensue. This not being the case, it is an obstacle. Also, the group operated in the days before the internet was truly established so communications were by letter, newsletters and the like through the postal system.

Were you always the Focaliser?

Up until the dissipation I did all the focalising, but it was planned for others to do so. The only reason it was I is that it was simply convenient, and I knew the process so well. Because this was the case there were others who had actually undertaken more Twelves than I had. This is not a requirement for future work and was only for the reason outlined. As long as a Focaliser had understood, and practiced the formation studiously, there is no reason why anyone could not undertake that role. In fact, for future work, it was thought that the role might be removed as it would be unnecessary if there were twelve highly trained and focussed participants.

From what did the Devic Presence and the Ashram protect you?

The Forces of Darkness are always seeking to disrupt those who work with Light. We were no different and used protection techniques to seal the formation as we worked. We were attacked, on occasion, but the onslaught was minimised and of nuisance value only. In fact I had more of this type of problem outside of the group than I ever had within it.

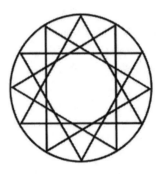

The Circle of Protection

The second thing is the securing of the energy within the formation. The protection was to keep the bad guys out and the good stuff in and it worked.

It is the contention of this book that this work is expansive and dynamic, and the Twelves is the next logical step in group work. Even if you are of a mind to disregard the experiences outlined in this book, I think there is true merit in considering the expansive nature of working in Twelve Formation. 2025 is fast approaching and we need all the tools we can muster to assist in breaking down old thoughtforms and clearing away channels for light to pour through. This is not an and/or scenario. This is in addition to the many aspects of group work, particularly of the Triangle Goodwill network, that is currently underway. Utilising the training and diligence that has been established on the inner planes, the beautiful thought-forms that have been created through that focussed effort.

Within this vast panorama of light work there is a place for focussed, laser-like work piercing the old and redundant thought-forms of yesteryear and opening channels of light, then through conscious attention, linking to those on the inner planes who seek to help humanity in this hour of crisis. As the switch was in off position there were never any consequences, with regards protection, in the daily lives of participants.

Can you explain a little more about The Vortex that was formed in the middle of the Twelve?

I think the best way to answer this is to quote DK as he describes, perfectly, what the funnel is and how it works:

"The first postulate to remember in considering the collective use of form in meditation is that those forms, in employing sound and rhythm, should open up a funnel of communication between those taking part in them and the intelligences or Powers they are seeking to approach. By means of this funnel which penetrates from the physical to the emotional or still higher to one or other of the mental levels. The Intelligences or powers are enabled to pour forth illuminating light or power of some kind or other into those who thus approach them. The funnel forms a channel whereby the contact can be made.

The whole process is purely scientific and is based on vibration and on a knowledge of dynamics. It is dependent upon the accurate formation, through occult knowledge, of a vacuum. The occult statement that "Nature abhors a vacuum" is entirely true. When through the correct intoning of certain sounds, this vacuum or empty funnel between the higher and lower is formed. Force pours into the funnel under the inevitable working of the law, and, via that funnel, reaches its objective.

Part of the power of the Hierarchy is based on their ability to do just this very thing. As evolution progresses, and the matter is more fully comprehended meditation groups will change from their present status, which is that of bands of earnest aspirants seeking illumination, to bands of workers constructively and intelligently working together for certain ends.

Another angle of the whole matter resolves itself into work in the world. Groups will apply themselves to the work of contacting certain types of logoic force, of passing it through the group funnel, and of sending it out through the world for certain constructive ends. This work is closely allied to that taken by the Nirmanakayas or the Distributors of Force, and will be largely under their direction, for They will be able to use these groups as focal points for Their activities."

Alice A. Bailey, *Letters on Occult Meditation*

As you can see, this is the very funnel that we formed and used during our Twelves work together. We illustrated ours like this:

The Funnel or Vortex

Minkowski's work with space and time correlates for the esotericist in a very meaningful way as his diagram describing distance/space and a funnel or vortex and the concentrated event in the middle relates exactly to the event that takes place in the middle of the funnel described by DK and the vortex described by the Twelves Group and experienced in their work.

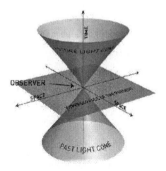

Minkowski's Funnel

Will you, personally, work with Twelves again?

I undertook Twelves work, somewhat reluctantly at first, as a service activity many years ago. I led the group with Robert and Peter over many years as we developed the process. It was both a joy and a burden and to do it properly we immersed ourselves within it. We all gained huge insights into ashramic process and huge insights into our own natures. We grew with it. Starting from those early years full of expectation and glamour we battled through it all. Don't forget, unwittingly, many in our own group encouraged some of those illusions and it took many years to get clarity. This is a long and arduous inner journey and I think I have attempted to do my part. This book is the last part of the jigsaw that I promised to fulfil to outline the background, process and outcomes. I hope that I have done that. I will not be leading any new group. That does not mean, however, that if such a serious group emerged that I would not assist in any way I can, including teaching the techniques required for successful Twelves, if asked. This is my commitment until it is time for me, too, to return home.

During the Twelves Group Gatherings did any of the participants sense, such as hear, see or smell, anything notable?

Yes, there were many experiences among the participants. Usually, the next day, we would sit in a circle and discuss and share our experiences of the Twelves the previous day. We did not encourage this on the day of the Twelve as the intensity was so great that we all wanted to be silent.

As we sat we shared our perspectives and the core experience of intense energy, connection and love was the same for us all. Some saw light, some heard bells and some were overcome with a fragrance of such beauty that they could hardly talk about it. It must be remembered that we were breaching the worlds and that the effect, upon each of us, was profound yet differed slightly. The core experience never differed and is very difficult to put into words.

I liken it to a vast reservoir of love and energy descending through the funnel and out through the participants, who undertook the role of facilitators, or channels. This energy was far greater than anything any of us had, or have, experienced. It just flowed when the group switch was thrown open.

Many of us felt that we could fly into the vast colours above the group formation and keep on flying into the heart of the ashram. It was immersive.

Tell us a bit more about the Bell you heard whilst seventeen.

That Bell was really a wake up call in the deepest sense. It is impossible to accurately reproduce this ethereal sound here on the earth plane but, after extensive research, I have found the closest match is a bell on the 417 Hz frequency on the Solfeggio Scale. But I must stress this is not a perfect reproduction but is the closest I have found.

The Solfeggio Scale has 6 tones (that is 6 'outer tones' and probably a reflected 6 'inner' tones' that undertake the deeper, healing work).

Each tone has a 'quality' and the 417 Hz is said to "facilitate change and allow any negative past to be healed and let go". The scale was originally developed by a Monk around 991-1050 AD and was utilized for chants, etc.

As I have said, the tone is not exact but the quality of 417 Hz frequency fits the situation. I was seventeen and had come through an abysmal childhood and, naturally, I had been deeply scarred. It makes sense that the ashram would initiate a healing so that I could proceed forward to the Twelves work.

I should state here that the childhood experience would have been karmic, a hastening of karma if you like, so that I could be fit for the experiment ahead. And so, the Bell cleansed and healed, although I was completely unaware of the importance of this until very recently when writing this book. I had always thought that it was just an opening of the psychic centers, but its significance was far more profound than that and explains why it was ubiquitous for weeks then never heard of again. But... I have never forgotten its tone and it is true to say that it has followed me all of this life.

This is a good place to mention that the Twelves Group also had a note or tone and our group OMs resonated in synergy even when we had imbalance in the formation. The older hands would carry and lift those less experienced and the result was synergy. This is another reason why we would break into the four triangles first, before the Twelves ritual, and get the note right between the three.

As described in Chapter 6 the formation came together in stages, 3, 6, 9, 12 and this raised the note of individuals and individual triangles utilising the OM as the synergistic tool.

"When the hearts of men as a whole are sufficiently open then will peace reign over all. Catch a flicker of that light from on high and reflect it."

The Initiate Feb 1982

Chapter Six

———◦———

A Manual for Group Workers (Reproduced for Completion and Written in the 1990s)

PART ONE

PURPOSE OF THE MANUAL: To provide a clearly outlined guide to assist Twelves Group light workers in the consistent implementation and activation of 12-pointed Stars; to ensure that all 12-pointed Stars energetically express and reflect the Twelves Group focus.

What is a Twelve?

The Twelve Group formation is twelve individuals working in specific star formation under the spiritual sponsorship and inspiration of a center within the Spiritual Hierarchy known as the ashram of the Brotherhood of the Star. This ashram is a center of light on the inner planes and is made up of masters, initiates and disciples who consciously choose to work with the regeneration of earth in cooperation with the forces of light including the angelic, devic, human and elemental realms.

Brief History of Twelves

The Twelves Group was started in 1990 and has grown from the initial work of the Order of the Star during the 1980s. The group, after much initial groundwork, undertook the first Twelve at Wesak, April 25th, 1994, in Glastonbury, England. A core group of seven men and five women participated in the activation of the first 12-pointed Star. The twelve members represented various countries including England, Scotland, Belgium, Holland, Canary Islands and the United States of America.

Potential Planetary Purposes for the Twelves Groups Work

As the Twelves Group strengthens its focus, enlarges its participation of light workers, and expands the number of Star Gatherings activations, it will be propelled more deeply into the Work of Twelves. The planetary purposes include the following: healing work with energy lines and major energy centers of the earth plane; cultural, political, social and financial structures; wielding of Ray energies, especially the three Major Rays; the transmutation of collective thought forms which no longer serve the evolutionary purpose of Planet earth; assisting the manifestation of the Christ onto the earth plane; assisting the Externalisation of the Spiritual Hierarchy and the work of the Brotherhood of the Star.

Mandatory Requirements for Twelves Work

Each light worker takes on the mantle of the Twelves Group by offering full attention and focus to the specific work of Twelves in a soul-conscious manner. Each light worker agrees to set aside the personality and other kinds of group work and activity throughout the time period of undertaking Twelves work. There is a commitment to be present from beginning to completion of the Work and to focus 100% on the Work in hand. It is vital to the success of this particular spiritual energetic work that other tools and methods of light work are not allowed to filter into the process of the Star Gatherings. This will provide quality assurance for the energetic resonance of our Work. We recognise that many Twelves group light workers may be involved as members and/or leaders of other spiritual groups and activities.

We applaud the many ways that light workers are contributing to the betterment of life on earth. We do ask that when you work with the group as a Twelves Group worker you honour and respect the purity of this specific group work.

Composition of a Twelve

Each Twelves Group is composed of twelve committed people and must include at least one core foundation member (this should be the Focaliser) in order for a Star Activation to be conducted (please note: a core member is one who has physically participated in at least two annual Star Gatherings).

PART TWO

Conducting a Twelve

Advance preparation for a Group Gathering:

Site selection: select a site conducive to the meditative work of the group. The site ideally should be a quiet, indoor location, on the ground floor if possible, with privacy for the entire time period of the Gathering. Ideally, you will be able to control the room temperature, air ventilation and lock the door leading into the room. Easy access to bathroom facilities is desirable.

Scheduling a Twelve

Schedule a Twelve at a monthly Full Moon or other appropriate time. Send notice of the Twelve to participants and include a detailed time schedule for the entire period of the Twelve including meals and breaks. Include advice that participants should honour the following: no heavy meals, no drugs and no alcohol in preparation for the Twelve.

Attuning to Purpose

When sending notification, please emphasise and encourage all workers to begin focussing, prior to The Twelve, on attunement with the spiritual purpose for the Twelve.

Focaliser's Responsibility and Purpose:

Each Twelve must have a Focaliser. The Focaliser's responsibility and purpose is to hold the group alignment with ashramic intent throughout the Twelve and to intuitively guide the Work of the Twelve, serving as the link between the Twelve and the ashram. This requires total selflessness and a willingness to soulfully serve the ashram with a mind and heart fully attentive to the directing influence of the ashram.

The Focaliser's Preparation

The Focaliser will set his/her own intent to align his/ her will with the Will of the ashram. The Focaliser will begin this preparation as soon as a Twelve is scheduled. The Focaliser will privately enter the Twelves site before the participants, allowing sufficient private time to thoroughly clear the energies present at the physical site and establish an energetically sacred space for the group work. The Focaliser will use his/her own particular esoteric cleanings practices to accomplish this task such as mantras, invocation, psychic clearing with sound (Tibetan bells), incense and smudging, etc.

The Focaliser will then seal the room through invocative command. This process must be completed before the group workers are granted admittance to the Gathering.

Individual Preparation

Each individual will focus on his/her own intent to serve prior to the Twelve. The individual, during meditations, will visualise all participants functioning as one Mind, one Heart, one Soul, in accord with the ashramic purpose. It is recommended that individuals lovingly care for their physical vehicles (sufficient rest, exercise, healthy foods and pure water) so that they have the physical stamina to channel the intense spiritual energies activated by a 12-pointed Star.

It is important that workers wear comfortable, loose fitting clothing during the Gatherings. It is an unspoken agreement that if you participate in a 12-pointed Star Gathering, you have committed to wear the Mantle of the Twelves Group. Be on time and on purpose.

Site Accessories

It is absolutely imperative that pure water be readily available at the Twelves site for all participants. Bottled spring water is best. Please be reminded that workers should drink lots of water throughout the duration of the meeting (but not actually in the Twelve). This is important because of higher energies pouring through the vehicle. Have floor cushions for participants. Also, have handouts such as "The Disciples Invocation", "The Great Invocation" and sign-in registration sheets. Please do not allow networking materials on the site. Any networking is requested to be done outside this dedicated environment. This request is made to prevent possible mixing of various thought-forms in an environment that has been cleared and sealed for the particular work of Twelves.

Other site Requirements

Please require that all footwear is removed at the entrance to the room. If the meeting sets a meditative focus in the center of the room such as a candle or incense, participants should respect this altar area by not walking through the center, rather walking around it.

Protective Work

The Focaliser must always open the meeting with a protective meditation. All meeting participants should be included, not only those who are actually going to take part in the Twelve. The Focaliser will ask participants to quiet themselves and visualise a globe of light in the middle of the room. Guiding the participants, the Focaliser then asks everyone to visualise points of light emerging from each (member) to the globe in the center of the room. From this center a pillar of light ascends to form a cone above which (about 12 feet/3.5 meters above the group) a protective Angelic Being is then sensed. From this Being of Light a shaft of light descends into the globe and, through waves of light in concentric circles, light flows around the room and forms a protective outer globe of light within which the meeting takes place.

If the meeting is more than one day, this should be repeated daily before work is undertaken. OMs should be used throughout this process to direct the light and visualisation.

PART THREE

The Work

All meditative 12-pointed Star Work is done standing, arms relaxed at the sides, feet firmly planted on the floor, eyes preferably closed. The body remains still with no extraneous movement during the Work.

Preparation

Establish a set marker for all 4 cardinal direction points, at the site, beginning with Cardinal Point North, then South, East and West. Always begin with the North point. The Focaliser must have a compass for this activity. Next, the Focaliser will intuitively, under ashramic guidance, select the twelve people to serve as the Star. This will be done by selecting and designating each Triangle of the Star:

First	Red Triangle – North
Second	Blue Triangle – South
Third	Green Triangle – East
Fourth	Yellow Triangle – West

(note: colours assigned to aid participants' memories only)

Ideally, each meeting should have twelve people serving in the Star formation and the Focaliser, in service outside the Star, as the facilitator. If there are only twelve workers present and this is not possible, the Focaliser should take up the North Triangle point position (this is always located on the magnetic compass direction).

Additional participants will serve as a protective and supportive energy circled around the Star without any identification with any particular Star point. These workers will be advised of their role and the opportunity for future work in which they may participate.

Rehearsal of Triangles

After selection of twelve people for the Star, determine three individuals for each Triangle beginning North, South, East then West. These individual Triangles will separate into their own groups around the room for a practice period. Each Triangle will designate one person as the Cardinal Anchor Point to lead the OMs and to be the Triangle sensor for energy linking. Each Triangle practices united resonating OMs led by their Anchor point person. A Twelve is not created when there are not Twelve participants--if there are less than 12 the focus should be on creating a 6-pointed Star which will pave the way for a later 12-pointed Star.

It is essential that after the Triangles have sufficient energy linkage and practice that they then form into a 6 to begin the process of stepping up the energies and to mesh the process into group work.

Rehearsal of Twelve-Pointed Star

All participants form a circle. Focaliser guides as follows: have each Triangle position themselves as the correct location of each Cardinal Point with the Anchor at the directional point. Beginning and identifying in order of 1st Red, 2nd Blue, 3rd Green, 4th Yellow. The first Triangle is instructed to step forward, then 2nd, 3rd, 4th. Thus, participants will understand their position within both the Triangle and the Star. All twelve then step back into a circle still holding their relative positions. Focaliser asks the participants to prepare for the Work and asks that the Work be for the good of all and that, through the ashram, all who need to be present for the Work are invited. Other workers present form the circle around the Twelve formation and participate by meditating and supporting the Twelve with love and light.

Activation

Focaliser will direct 1st Triangle to take position. Focaliser holds spiritual energetic concentration as 1st moves into position. When 1st Triangle is in position Focaliser asks participants to visualise a Point of Light leaving their heart center and joining with their co-workers' creating a Triangle of Light at chest height. Focaliser sensing linkage asks the Triangle Point to lead three OMs visualising this light between the Triangle participants

N

First Triangle

The 1st Triangle maintains attunement in position. Next Focaliser directs 2nd Triangle to step forward and take position. The 2nd Triangle centers and energetically links. Participants are asked by the Focaliser to visualise a Point of Light about 3 inches about the 1st Triangles lightwork. When Focaliser sense and recognises linking complete, Focaliser requests 2nd Triangle Anchor Point to lead 3 OMs (sounded by 2nd Triangle only).

The Focaliser now asks Triangle 2 to lower their Triangle of Light and Triangle 1 to raise their Triangle of Light so that the 2 Triangles of light meet and merge into a 6-pointed Star. Triangle 1 and 2 are now attuned and will continue to hold that attunement.

When the Focaliser senses merging between the two Triangles is complete, the Focaliser requests the North Point Anchor to lead both Triangles in the sounding of 3 OMs simultaneously. Now there is an energy pattern of a 6-pointed Star as the merged Triangles hold and maintain this attunement. Focaliser voices confirmation of this merged energy

N

S

Second Triangle.

Next, the Focaliser calls forth 3rd Triangle which then steps forward into position with Triangles 1 and 2. When 3rd Triangle's points have linked (through the same process as the first two) then the Focaliser asks the East Anchor Point to lead with 3 OMs for 3rd Triangle only.

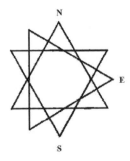

Third Triangle

Then the 3rd Triangle merges and blends energy about three inches above the 6-pointed Star and, at the Focalisers direction, the 6-pointed Star raises its energy and the 3rd Triangle lowers their energy until the 9-pointed Star is formed. Thus the 6-pointed Star becomes a 9-pointed Star. When merging and blending complete the Focaliser asks the North Anchor Point (1st Triangle) to sound the 3 OMs which are enjoined by all 9 in the Star completing the blending. Focaliser voices affirmation that the 9 is complete.

Then the 4th Triangle merges and blends energy with the 9-pointed Star in the same way and a Twelve Pointed Star is formed.

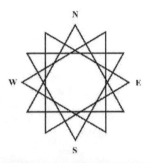

The Completed Twelve

When the Focaliser senses that this energetic merging is complete he/she asks the North Point to now lead all points (all 12 participants) in 3 OMs.

The energy of all 4 Triangles is blended, circulating and entwining in twelve completely activated points. All twelve hold the energy intact. Each heart center activates, and the energy centered in each heart is projected into the center of the Star Formation in a focussed manner creating a Chalice of Light which ascends to about 12 feet (3.5 meters) above the group.

The Devic presence overlighting the twelve-pointed Star responds through the Chalice by pouring light and energy down into the focus ready for work.

As these Rays of Light reach the center of the twelve-pointed Star, the rays blend and merge, spiralling and joining as the rays move upwards in a spiral movement forming a Light Vortex which intensifies and converges about 12 feet (3.5 meters) above the group formation.

It then expands or diverges upward into a Chalice of Light. This energetic building and intensification of Light elicits a Devic response. The Focaliser asks the group formation to acknowledge this Devic response with love. Now the group formation has been energetically prepared to link with the ashram. The Focaliser makes and voices that link for all the group and there is a response from the ashram.

As this group link with the ashram is formed, the Focaliser asks the group to focus on the ashramic energy and become available for the Work. The Focaliser now undertakes the Work requesting the cooperation of the group formation, the Hierarchy and the Angelic Devic Presence to participate in the alchemical energetic flow. The Work is commanded by the voicing of the Focaliser.

Note: The Work is undertaken and led by the Focaliser-- often specific work has been requested by the ashram or it can be a general light bearing and focussing work for the planet.

Withdrawal

Upon completion of the Work, the Focaliser returns the energetic focussed attention of the group formation in this manner:

"Now we begin to withdraw. We return to the ashram and Devic presence overlighting the Twelve. We withdraw our focus back from the Work, returning to our group focus within the vortex of the funnel."

When the group consciousness has returned to the Vortex, the Focaliser will state the completion of the work by directing: "We will withdraw from the formation."

The Focaliser continues to guide the withdrawal of the group, step-by-step, in a clear, loving, and unhurried manner, remaining attentive to the group. Expressing gratitude and thanksgiving, withdraw from ashramic contact whilst remaining within the shelter of the overlighting Devic presence. With gratitude and thanksgiving, withdraw the group formation contact with that presence.

Slowly withdraw, untwining the vortex energies and returning to the heart of the group Star. Begin untwining all of the Twelve strands by, staring with the 4th Triangle lift off the Triangle of Light above the others and step back into the original position. When this has been achieved by all 4 Triangles the Focaliser leads the

Twelve in reciting the Great Invocation leading the final 3 OMs by all members of the group present.

Maintaining Sacred Space

Upon completion of this powerful energetic work, maintain great respect for the heightened sensitivity and vulnerability of each light worker. Allow each one to reintegrate with ordinary reality at their own pace. The room should be maintained as a sacred space for silence, private meditation (and no physical contact) for a prearranged period of time (probably an hour, at least). This sacred space must be honoured by all. It is our experience that most people do not want to talk and want to go their own way for the rest of that day or at least for a few hours.

Re-integration with humanity: The day following a Star Activation is time for sharing the experience together and closing down and removing items from the sacred space. Often, we have dinner on the last night to share our experiences before we each depart to our homes.

It is important the participants have grounding time. Quite often at Gatherings participants have wanted to go off into nearby fields just to rest and lay on the earth to allow the Chakras to ground again and let go of excess energy.

Note

The above Manual for Twelves was written by the group in the 1990s and we followed this format as the years went by. We did make certain adjustments in the very early Twelves, for example, adding colour codes for the differing four triangles to make it simpler for participants to remember their positions during the very intense energies that abounded.

The actual formation had to be fixed so that participants were certain of their role and were prepared for it. What we could not control, of course, was the ashramic response nor the energy flow. We were instructed to work with the three cities mentioned earlier to break down thought forms and build a bridge of light and healing. Our foremost role was to build the funnel that DK talks about in Chapter Five.

The energy Vortex was very real and was felt, and sometimes seen by those present. It is a testament to the Work that participants had this very real experience and connection and is also why the group's core members, often experiencing great financial sacrifice, flew around the world to attend and be a part of this historic experiment. It is difficult to impart to those not present, the powerful presence of light, energy and power. This was not produced by the participants, of course, but was entirely of ashramic origination as they sought to use the Twelve, or at least, prepare the Twelve for potential use.

It would be easy to dismiss participants' experiences as that of the imagination, but one must remember that many of those present were experienced esotericists of many years standing and not easily caught up in glamorous activities of no substance. We had trained members from most of the large, well established schools of the ancient wisdom although the majority were from the Lucis Trust and those organisations closely allied to it.

To be there was to be present. Unfolding before us was real, dynamic and powerful group synthesis and group working. To be cynical and doubtful is natural and, actually, if balanced, to be encouraged in many respects. Readers are also requested to respect those that took part were also of the same frame of mind and many times we all doubted what laid before us--until it happened. And when it happened doubt soon left us as a distant memory, and we all got on with the job.

"Four square They will stand and the Three will utter the Word and the One shall make it Law"

The Initiate March 1982

Chapter Seven

Original Afterword

AND SO IT began and was finished: a neat little esoteric package where brave men and women gallantly stepped onto the group stage to attempt what had never been attempted before--direct, under the guidance, and instructed by, an ashram on the inner planes. They, as much as us, were attempting contact and add further cooperation within that great thrust of the externalisation. A small droplet in that ocean can but be a part of it, nonetheless.

Much has been talked about, written about and discussed between esoteric workers of the times to come, the Aquarian Age, New Age, call it what thou wilt. This time is foreseen by many traditions and hoped for by many a human being. In many ways it is a new Restoration, or maybe a better term is a new renaissance of a time upon our earth when peace and goodwill reign.

It is our birth right and our destiny but to get there humanity has to learn to cooperate more, to work together in synthesis and to bridge that gap between the unseen and the seen for in bridging that gap can continuance of life be known, cooperation between realms understood and the unity in all things be grasped.

It does not take a genius to observe the world as it is now. We lurch between crises, political, social and environmental. Questions constantly arise, "Where shall we go?". "To whom shall we seek guidance and advice?" "Can we do it alone?"

In many ways' humanity is an experiment itself. There are no guarantees, no certainties and this makes us all feel the cold shudders of insecurity. We seek the solace in many a thing to help us deal with day to day life which seems to change constantly. When one crisis stops, another unfolds, then another and another.

Humanity has been given the tools to break this cycle and many teachings have been given to us that inform us of our part in invoking change ahead of a chance at redemption for us all. All religions talk of this.

They all talk of a Coming One whether He be called the Christ, the Messiah, Maitreya, Krishna or the Imam Mahdi, it is obvious it is one and the same. The issue is, "Will He just turn up?" and "We don't have to do anything?" It is a bit like 'shall we just wait with the certain knowledge that He will come, eventually, knocking upon the world's door?'.

Theosophy, that great gamut of knowledge that strides science, religion, philosophy and the arts teach us slightly differently. Starting with Helena Blavatsky who laid the foundations with her Magnum Opus *The Secret Doctrine* through to the following great strands of light that expanded upon the good Madam's foundation; Alice

A. Bailey and Helena Roerich (principally Helena apart from the volume *Leaves of Morya's Garden* which was transmitted through her great initiate husband, Nicholas).

These three great initiates carried that torch of the Ancient Wisdom for all of us that were to follow, and they gave us insights and knowledge concerning our future and, specifically, how to influence it. This is the crux of it, the future, like the great law of karma, can be influenced and changed because it is DYNAMIC it is not static nor is it predestined.

There is no set-in stone fate that awaits us, no written down destiny that beckons us from some distant shore that we cannot change, alter or influence. All is flux and the state of the coming generations and of the planet itself is within our own hands.

But how do we proceed? Prayer alone is not enough and in the spirit of "God helps those who help themselves" we must proceed to establish rapport with those forces that might help us.

It has already been outlined that the work of DK is the perfect place to study concerning the New Group of World Servers and the Great Invocation and how, through working in Groups of Three (aka Triangles), great strides have and will be made to ensure a link is established, in broad terms, with the inner forces of light. Through Invocation response can be found and help proffered.

What this book sets out to achieve is that within that great endeavour is it not reasonable to assume that a more focussed, more direct and hence a more powerful connection could be made? I ask you to ponder on the possibility. It may be that you have read the story outlined and you have doubts as to some of the experiences recounted. They are, after all, in many ways, extraordinary and might be considered farfetched by some who are unfamiliar with this paradigm.

Maybe or maybe not, but this is unimportant as those that took part have their own experience and those that read here have theirs, each can decide for themselves, but the larger, expanding point is bearing down upon us like some glacier about to shear. Can direct, sustained and focussed contact be made with the Hierarchy, through the inner ashram, and can this work be enhanced by working in Groups of Twelve?

It's a simple enough reflection, it is either a yes or no. Even if large parts of the experiment are disregarded as fanciful is the concept viable? Taking into account the history over thousands of years regarding the importance of the number twelve and the known magical basis for group work (including Triangles etc.)

I have sought to outline why working in Twelves reflects cosmic proportions. I have outlined, albeit briefly, the references in every world religion and the supporting evidence from DK I also pointed out the prophecy from the Master Morya regarding Groups of Twelve in the book *Agni Yoga* and so it can be seen that the evidence, hints and documented structure around Twelves is as broad as it is long. Now...is it time?

I have also sought to give you a flavour of the work we did in the Twelves Group, with no claim for bright successes. I have just recorded what happened, as I, and others, experienced it. The outcome (as far as I could record the outcomes as most of it was inner work and I do not have the skills to record, nor even have great knowledge, of it) is as recorded here. All I can offer is, what happened is what happened.

And what of now? Well, this work was a long time ago and I let it go for a number of years whilst I focussed on my career and weighing myself down with academic study plus, even worse, weighing myself down with material career politics. But like that distant Bell that, once struck, continues its resonance this has never left me nor the vibration ever ceased. Hierarchical work is like that, once touched by the Masters' ashram it cannot be undone.

What seems to us like years, decades, time etc. is, in fact, relatively the twinkling of an eye. Evolution and karma continue and is dynamic and never stops, shuts down nor fades.

And, so here we are writing what needs to be recorded, a form of closure and, more importantly a form of beginning, a form of solidifying that which was fluid and ephemeral.

I hope I have captured that particular butterfly, that I have been gentle and released it with honesty, integrity and peace.

"Become as a lantern in the midst of time that some may see your friendly light flickering and may light their own candles from yours"

The Initiate June 1982

Chapter Eight

———◦◦◦———

We Start the Implementation Stage

IN THE early part of the work we were informed that our Twelves work would be in three stages:

1/ Preparation

2/ Implementation

3/ Revelation

The first stage, as we can see, was from 1980 to 2000 and involved receiving instructions from The Initiate and experimenting, in physical groups. This was partially successful, and it was felt, at the time, that there would be a lengthy gap between the first and second stage that would not involve a cross-over of coworkers. In fact, I had, in the First Edition of this book indicated that I had recorded the history and my part was finished and I laid it before the esoteric movement for others to take up in the future. I was wrong.

I retired to Asia in 2008 with documenting in mind. In fact, there was a substantial gap between settling in Asia and starting to write up the book in 2018. Not long after I started t reestablish my link to the ashram and I was made aware that the world was in crisis and hiding for the rest of my incarnation within Asia's bosom was my right of free will but not my Master's choice. With some reluctance I understood that I must work again with this experiment and the connection grew.

As I have stated in '*2025 and The World Teacher* (now largely incorporated in this new edition) I perceive that humanity is lagging far behind what was expected and planned and action and focus is needed urgently.

It might seem odd to the occasional esotericist but numbers, to achieve occult aims, can be relatively small. As little as three "gathered in my name" can have impact and it is my view that the triangle work through, primarily, Lucis Trust has actually saved this world from even greater horrors and continues to provide trained esotericists from which we, and other groups, might reap future focused coworkers.

We have rebooted the Twelves work to respond to this urgency. At this time (July 2019), we have two functional Twelves (24 coworkers) and will seek to expand that when the timing is appropriate. What is meant by that? It is two-fold:

1/ when we have committed, focused and functioning coworkers to can populate a Twelve

and

2/ when we have those coworkers responding to the ashram's call and need.

Sheer numbers is not what our small group is about. There is no point in having one hundred Twelves that are weak and ineffective. Twelves is an esoteric science and is not for everyone. It takes commitment, focus, clarity of purpose and TIME. We ask for every participant to have read this book, be willing belong to a triangle and undertake linkage with The Great Invocation daily, undertake monthly Full Moon Twelves and occasional (often weekly) Ashram Meditations. All of our coworkers are fully engaged with other esoteric work, that is encouraged, but being ready and 'in the present' with our particular work is essential and so we ask all to think very carefully before committing.

The new Twelves manifestation is populated by serious esoteric workers and we are very humbled by the quality. We have members from the Lucis Trust, Agni Yoga Society, University of the Seven Rays, Theosophical Society and many other New Group of World Server organisations.

You are welcome to enquire and invited to browse our new web site:

www.TwelveStar.org

We have been asked a few times for some clarification regarding Distant (absent, virtual or remote) Twelves and the physical version we undertook over many years.

I fear I have added to the intrigue unintentionally as originally in this book (page 99) I stated:

"Twelves could not be undertaken virtually as it had a specific ritual-based focus. It would be like an orchestra playing a symphony without being able to see the conductor nor hear the other players. It might produce some noise, and some sort of tune, but not quite what the composer had in mind."

This still holds true in much the same way as experienced Triangle workers can intuit the absence of partners within their Triangle if it has been agreed to meet' at an exact time. We know that it is not a requirement to undertake Triangles at exact times but the difference if definitely felt if one is undertaking the work correctly. The energy service work is enhanced by proper coordination and timing and it is difficult to deny this or explain it away as unimportant. Three main points:

1. Physical Twelves will exponentially be more powerful than Distant Twelves as will Physical Triangles as focus and coordination is easier. We realise that coordinating Triangles at exact times is a challenge and Distant Twelves would prove to even harder (but not impossible). The Formations we build on the inner planes remain and are there to be utilised and do not rely on all coworkers being there at the same time.

2. Distant Twelves can have huge impact. We have revaluated the potential of Distant Twelves in this new Implementory Stage and although recognise that physical presence adds to the focus, we now cognize that physical presence was essential to the first phase of preparation and learning but less so now.

3. Whilst I was writing the original book, I felt it was the end of my participation in the preparation aspect of The Work and that others would come, at some future date, and take up the Banner once more and implement

it. I was wrong. I have been asked to participate, once again, and my commitment is to do this until my dying breath, and I shall do so. We should make it clear that ashramic work is only sponsored if it is useful. Group work is always experimental and there is no guarantee of success. The work we do can have great impact or it can be held-over for others to take up again, once more, at a future time. I was, also, asked to reconsider my stubborn stance on Distant Twelves at the Preparatory Stage as this methodology is applicable, useful and relevant NOW. The work was introduced to us as three stages:

"I must make plain that the first stage is Preparatory, the second Implementory and the third Revelatory."

The Initiate May 1982

Even though the coworker membership has changed this is not of note. The energy work we undertook set the calibration of our work ahead. This was undertaken successfully, mostly, and the Preparatory stage has been completed. We must now dust down that first stage, restart the motor and begin the Implementory Stage.

One of the first challenges is finding the sleepers, those that are fit for this work, our ashramic friends and coworkers who have come here, just as we have, to help our planet prepare for 2025 and beyond there is NO GREATER task set before us. We must act, and act we will, together onward answering and echoing The Call.

"Be as Still as the Lilly in the Pond"

The Initiate 1979

Chapter Nine

The Conclaves: 1425 to 1825

1425

IN THIS year the Great Assembly made the manifestation of a huge leap in human consciousness the prime focus for its work. Prior to 1425 darkness had enveloped the world since Atlantean times.

"A great change in the human consciousness made it possible—in the year 1425 A.D.—to inaugurate changes in the requirements for initiation and definitely to lift the standard. Five hundred years have gone by since then, and the purpose of these changes in discipline and training have proved well warranted. In spite of all signs to the contrary, in spite of the world war with its attendant horrors and in spite of the apparent unawakened attitude of the masses, a very real measure of monadic energy is present."

Djwhal Khul, *Discipleship in the New Age Vol.2,* p.269

Djwhal Khul

"For some time, ever since 1425 A.D., (a date to which I referred earlier) the Hierarchy has been aware that the time would come when this projected move would take place. Preparations have gone steadily forward. A point to be remembered is that this impulsed intention (emanating in the first place from Shamballa) came as a major disturbance to the rhythm of many tens of thousands of years; it has been a basic conditioning factor. The Masters, however, who will make the move outwards into contact with the world are not the Ones Who registered the initial impulse from Shamballa, nor are the three Heads of the great departments the same. The earlier Masters initiated the needed steps of preparation, and the work has gone steadily forward since. "

Djwhal Khul, *The Externalization of the Hierarchy,* p. 568

Ray Three came into manifestation via The Lord of Active Intelligence and this stimulated the slow transmutation of matter and the creating of a more advanced humanity.

"This third ray has been in objective manifestation since 1425 A.D. and will remain in incarnation throughout the Aquarian Age. Its cycles are the longest of any of the ray cycles. However, within these major cycles there are periods of intensified activity which are like the beat or pulsation of the heart and these periods last approximately three thousand years."

Djwhal Khul, *The Destiny of the Nations,* p. 136

"Ray Three: in manifestation since 1425 A.D."

Djwhal Khul, *Esoteric Psychology Vol.1,* p. 26

"One of the tasks which I have undertaken is to awaken the aspirants and the disciples of the world to the new possibilities and to the new incoming potencies which can become available for use, if they will pass on to a fuller grasp of the developments since 1425 A.D."

Djwhal Khul, *Discipleship in the New Age Vol.2,* p. 270

The Great Invocation was first used in 1425 by the Hierarchy at the Great Assembly and has been used ever since as a very real tool for world advancement. In 1945 it was given to humanity to use daily and has now been translated into 80 languages and dialects.

"This Great Invocation has been used by the Hierarchy ever since the year 1425 A.D. though it is thousands of years older than that. Owing, however, to the unreadiness of humanity to cooperate in its use, the results have been delayed and are regarded as hovering.

I know not how else to express the results already achieved. Today, they can precipitate, if right cooperation can be extended by humanity, and such cooperation now seems immediately possible."

Djwhal Khul, *The Externalisation of the Hierarchy,* p. 158

"When the Hierarchy withdrew behind the separating curtain in Atlantean times, it marked the beginning of an interlude of darkness, of aridity and a cycle of "blank abstraction," which persisted in its crudest form until 1425 A.D., and since then has sensibly lightened until we reached the year 1925."

Djwhal Khul, *Discipleship in the New Age Vol.2,* p. 316

1525

The only thing of note is that there were "certain difficulties" in 1525 mentioned by DK in *Esoteric Psychology 2,* p. 261.

1625

We now jump to 1625 as there is no useful information regarding 1525 other than "certain difficulties"

Djwhal Khul, *Esoteric Psychology Vol.2,* p. 261.

At the Conclave in 1625 Djwhal Khul mentions which are of note:

"Today, as a result of a spiritual awakening which dates from 1625 A.D., and which laid the emphasis upon a wider, general education and upon a revolt from the imposition of clerical authority, the radiation from the world of souls has greatly intensified and the Kingdom of God is becoming a corporate part of the outer world expression, and this for the first time in the long, long history of humanity."

Djwhal Khul, *Discipleship in the New Age Vol.2,* p. 407

Ray 6 began to pass out in 1625 and we can assume that was the beginning of the end for the Piscean Era.

"The sixth ray began to pass out of manifestation in 1625 after a long period of influence, whilst the seventh Ray of Ceremonial Order began to come into manifestation in 1675."

Djwhal Khul, *The Destiny of the Nations,* p. 29

1725

It appears at this Conclave the Masters were concerned with not unduly influencing mankind as They were concerned with avoidance of impacting free will.

"Even in connection with the uncertain activities of mankind, the Masters can usually gauge what will occur, but esoterically They refuse 'to ponder on the energies released upon the plane of earthly living, for fear that counter-energies, issuing from the Centre where They dwell may negate the truth of man's freewill. I am here quoting one of the Masters, speaking at a conference held in 1725."

Djwhal Khul, *Esoteric Healing,* p. 380

We are told that a raft of incarnating souls took physical incarnation early to avert problems which had existed since 1525. This had positive and negative effects, some of which, in scientific developments, were used for evil effects.

"About the beginning of the eighteenth century, after a meeting of the Hierarchy at its great centennial gathering in 1725, an effort was determined upon which would bring a more definite influence to bear upon a group of souls awaiting incarnation, and thus induce them to hasten their entry into the life of the physical plane. This was done, and the civilisation of modern times came into being, with both good and bad results.

The era of culture which was the outstanding characteristic of the Victorian age, the great movements which awakened the human consciousness to a recognition of its essential freedom, the reaction against the dogmatism of the Church, the great and wonderful scientific developments of the immediate past, and the present sexual and proletarian revolutions now going on, are the result of the impulsive' hastenings into incarnation of souls whose time had not truly come but whose conditioning influence was needed if certain difficulties (present since 1525) were to be averted.

The bad effects above mentioned are indicative of the difficulties incident to premature development and to the undesirable unfoldment's of what might be termed (injudiciously nevertheless) evil."

Djwhal Khul, *Esoteric Psychology Vol.2*, p. 260

It appears that not all Masters are members of the Conclave and Djwhal Khul here mentions the sounding of the 'O' by Sanat Kumara at these Conclaves:

"It will therefore be apparent to you inferentially, how comparatively few of the Members of our Hierarchy have yet been able to reach the state or condition of development which would warrant Their forming a part of the great Council, or which would enable them to respond to the O, sounded out at intervals of one hundred years by Sanat Kumara. It is this sound which gathers together the responsive Units into the Council. This Council is held at one hundred year intervals, and as far as our modern humanity is concerned, these Councils have been held— under our arbitrary dates—in 1725, 1825, 1925."

Djwhal Khul, *The Rays and Initiations, p.* 206

1825

This Conclave heralded Second Ray Initiates and disciples beginning the outpouring of Christ Consciousness into the world and hence the formation of labour movements and welfare organisations.

"I refer to the outpouring of the Christ consciousness and the spirit of love upon the world. This was initiated in

1825, and brought about the major welfare movements, led to the organisation of the groups which wrought for human betterment, aided in the founding of the labour movements which were founded on right motive, inspired educational processes, philanthropic enterprises and the great medical expansions, and which today is seeping into world government and beginning to condition all the plans for world peace and international relations. Success is assured, though movements may progress slowly...."

Djwhal Khul, *Discipleship in the New Age Vol.2,* p. 592

"The Hierarchy also had to take into account the decreasing power of the Second Ray which partially led to the world wars.

Therefore in 1825 the potency of this ray began to decline as the peak of its two hundred fifty years emergence was reached. It was the gradual withdrawal of this ray which led to that growth of separativeness in the world which produced the European wars and the great World War."

Djwhal Khul, *Esoteric Psychology Vol.1,* p. 349

The largest event of the 1825 Conclave was, for the first time, allowing Shamballa to have a direct connection with earth and not via the Hierarchy. This, in fact, was a large experiment which we are still living with today and this powerful energy raises the best in us along with and the worst. Similarly as humans progress on the Initiatory Path karma speeds up and so it is with our earth's karmic progression.

"At this time, the work of the Great Council at Shamballa, working until now through the Hierarchy, is with the life within the form; They have to proceed with the utmost caution as They thus work, because these Lights know that the danger of premature direct contact with humanity, and of consequent overstimulation, are great.

One of the causes of the present cataclysm is the fact that humanity was deemed capable of taking and receiving a 'touch from Shamballa,' without stepping it down via the Hierarchy, as has hitherto been the custom. The determination to apply this touch (which is in the nature of a great experiment) was made in 1825, when the Great Council had its usual centennial meeting... All has been speeded up and little such growth was seen on a worldwide scale prior to 1825."

Djwhal Khul, *The Rays and The Initiations,* p. 145

"All these changes have been due to the successful response of our planetary life, expressed through the human kingdom at this time, to the processes of evolution and to the inflow (since 1825) of the will energy from Shamballa. This, in its turn, is due to the progress of Sanat Kumara Himself, within His Own identified life upon the cosmic Path which emerges from the cosmic mental plane."

Djwhal Khul, *The Rays and The Initiations,* p. 412

"This period started in the year 1825 and will continue until the end of this century"

Djwhal Khul, *The Rays and The Initiations,* p. 571

When this Shamballic energy impacted our earth, after 1825, much evil was aroused and was burned for the greater, longer good. This was needed to ensure the externalisation and Reappearance of The World Teacher was unimpeded. Again there is correlation to individual human's progress on the Path of Discipleship where we all have to face the burning ground and The Dweller on the Threshold.

"When this direct line of spiritual, dynamic, electrical energy made its first impact on earth (after the Great Council held in 1825), it first of all awakened men's thinking in a new and comprehensive way, producing the great ideologies; it aroused their massed desire, and registered obstruction on the physical plane. It found its course impeded and discovered it was faced with barriers.

This energy from Shamballa, being an aspect of the ray of the destroyer, proceeded to burn up in the fires of destruction, all such hindrances upon the planes in the three worlds. This was the deeply esoteric and unrecognised cause of the war—the beneficent bringing to an end of the impediments to the free flow of spiritual energy down into the third centre; this was the factor which called "evil from its hidden place" and brought the opposing forces to the surface of existence, prior to their sealing'

The agents of the second ray started their preparation around the year 1825 and moved outward in force soon after 1860. From that date on, great concepts and new ideas, and the modern ideologies and arguments for and against aspects of the truth, have characterised modern thought and produced the present mental chaos and the many conflicting schools and ideologies, with their attendant movements and organisations; out of all these, order and truth and the new civilisation will emerge.

This civilisation will emerge as the result of mass thinking; it will no longer be a civilisation 'imposed' by an oligarchy of any kind. This will be a new phenomenon and one for which the Hierarchy has had to wait, prior to reappearing."

Djwhal Khul, *The Externalisation of the Hierarchy,* p. 678

"Blest are the feet of he who is on the path, blest are the hands of he who offers them in Brotherhood, blest is the mouth of he who speaks Truth, blest are the ears of he who hears the whisperings of the Word."

The Initiate 1982

Chapter 10

The Conclaves: 1925 to 2025

1925

THIS CONCLAVE made several far-reaching decisions regarding the externalisation. In many ways this Conclave was the most important one of all as it preceded 2025 and the Reappearance of The World Teacher. Thus several major decisions were to be taken which included the formation of subsidiary ashrams which included The Brotherhood of the Star which is an amalgamated ashram headed by Koot Hoomi and made up of Senior Initiates and Disciples, of various Ray ashrams, who have come together to work for the externalisation and Reappearance of The World Teacher.

"Senior disciples in the major Ashrams are now beginning to form subsidiary Ashrams, as I began to do in the year 1925"

Djwhal Khul, *Discipleship in the New Age Vol.2,* p. 64

"The steps taken at the Conclave in Shamballa in 1925 (based on tentative conclusion at the previous centennial Conclave) and the pressures exerted by the Hierarchy have proved most successful, and out of the chaos of the world war (precipitated by humanity itself) there is developing a structure of truth and a paralleling responsiveness of the human mechanism which guarantees the perpetuation and the rapid unfoldment of the next stage of the teaching of the Ageless Wisdom."

Djwhal Khul, *Discipleship in the New Age Vol.2,* p. 314

"When the Hierarchy withdrew behind the separating curtain in Atlantean times, it marked the beginning of an interlude of darkness, of aridity and a cycle of "blank abstraction," which persisted in its crudest form until 1425 A.D., and since then has sensibly lightened until we reached the year 1925."

Djwhal Khul, *Discipleship in the New Age Vol.2,* p. 316

"This process has been greatly facilitated since the entire Hierarchy shifted its location (since 1925 A.D.) from the higher mental levels to the buddhic plane, thereby making direct and unimpeded etheric reception possible."

Djwhal Khul, *Discipleship in the New Age Vol.2,* p. 405

As part of this outreach from 1925 two major decisions were made in the way ashrams and the Hierarchy interact with humanity and the formation of The New Group of World Servers (NGWS). The NGWS was to be a reflection of The Brotherhood of the Star and its members were from all Rays working in unison.

"In *A Treatise on White Magic* I outlined one of the first steps taken by the Hierarchy in the work of inaugurating the new Plan. This Plan was tentatively formulated in 1900, at one of the great quarterly meetings of the

Hierarchy. In 1925, at the next great meeting for cooperation, the new Plan was discussed in greater detail, certain necessary changes (growing out of the results of the World War) were negotiated, and the members of that important Council determined two things:

First, that there should be a united effort by the collective members of the planetary Hierarchy, over a period of several years (that is until 1950), to bring about certain definite results, and that during that time the attention of the Great Ones should be turned towards a definite attempt to expand the consciousness of humanity and to institute a sort of forcing process, so that men's horizon of thought would be tremendously enlarged, and their faith, assurance and knowledge be equally increased and strengthened. It was decided that certain areas of doubt should be cleared up.

Secondly, it was determined to link more closely and subjectively the senior disciples, aspirants and workers in the world. To this end, all the Masters put Their personal groups of disciples in touch with each other, subjectively, intuitively, and sometimes telepathically. Thus the New Group of World Servers came into being."

Djwhal Khul, *Esoteric Psychology Vol.1,* p170

"It is the work of the Ray of Magical Order which will bring about sensitivity to one of the Major Approaches which is being now attempted. Only as history is made and we learn later the amazing nature of the epoch through which the race is passing, will humanity appreciate the significance of the work of the present Hierarchy, and the magnitude and the success of its achievement since 1925, as a result of the initial impulse instituted in 1875."

Djwhal Khul, *Esoteric Psychology Vol.2,* p. 273

"However, if we could look on, as can Those on the inner side and if we were in a position to contrast the "light" of humanity as it is today with what it was two or three hundred years ago, we would recognise that enormous strides had been made. This is evidenced by the fact that the emergence of a band of 'conditioning souls', under the name of the New Group of World Servers, has been possible since 1925. They can now come in because of the work already done by the group of souls who hastened their entrance into incarnation, under the impulse of the Hierarchy."

Djwhal Khul, *Esoteric Psychology Vol.2,* p. 261

"Much however depends upon the aspirants and the disciples in the world at this time. The past year has been one of the world's worst experiences from the standpoint of agony and distress; the point of acutest suffering has been reached. It has, however, been the year in which the greatest spiritual Approach of all time has shown itself to be possible—an Approach for which the initiates and Masters have for centuries been preparing, and for which all the Wesak Festivals since the meeting of the Great Council in 1925 have been preparatory. I have, in past instructions, referred to the great meetings held at intervals by Those to Whom is entrusted the spiritual guidance of the planet and particularly of man."

Djwhal Khul, *The Externalisation of the Hierarchy,* p. 389

"The stimulation which was set up and the light which was permitted to creep through after the last hierarchical conclave in 1925 has been real and effective. That meeting of the Masters of the Wisdom upon spiritual levels led to three results or happenings, and these we are today experiencing.

The first was a fresh inflow of the Christ principle of spiritual or true love which is ever free from emotionalism and selfish intent. This inflow resulted in the immediate and rapid growth of all movements towards peace, world understanding, goodwill, philanthropic effort and the awakening of the masses of men to the issues of brotherhood.

The second was the stimulation of the principle of relationship and this led to the growth and the perfecting of all sources of inter-communication such as the press, the radio and travel. The inner objective of all this was to bring human beings closer together upon the outer plane of existence and thus parallel objectively the developing inner, spiritual unity.

The third was the inflow of the force of *will or power* from the Shamballa centre. This, as previously explained, is the most powerful force in the world today, and only twice before in the history of mankind has this Shamballa energy made its appearance and caused its presence to be felt through the tremendous changes which were brought about."

Djwhal Khul, *The Externalisation of the Hierarchy,* p. 106

"All these projects if carried forward under Hierarchical inspiration and in a spirit of true humility and understanding are contributory to the factors in a great spiritual enterprise which the Hierarchy started in 1925."

Alice A. Bailey, *The Unfinished Autobiography,* p. 230

The year 1925 was also the year *A Treatise on Cosmic Fire* was published:

"In many ways today Helena Petrovna Blavatsky's (H.P.B.) book *The Secret Doctrine* is out of date and its approach to the Ageless Wisdom has little or no appeal to the modern generation. But those of us who really studied it and arrived at some understanding of its inner significance have a basic appreciation of the truth that no other book seems to supply. H.P.B. said that the next interpretation of the Ageless Wisdom would be a psychological approach, and *A Treatise on Cosmic Fire*, which I published in 1925, is the psychological key to *The Secret Doctrine*. None of my books would have been possible had I not at one time made a very close study of *The Secret Doctrine*."

Alice A. Bailey, *The Unfinished Autobiography,* p. 214

2025

And so, we arrive (nearly) at 2025. *A Treatise on Cosmic Fire* (published in that Conclave year 1925) is the foundation teaching towards 2025:

"...it also presented the psychological key to *The Secret Doctrine* and is intended to offer study to disciples and initiates at the close of this century and the beginning of the next century, up until 2025 A.D."

Djwhal Khul, *Discipleship in the New Age Vol.1,* p. 778

"Above everything else required at this time is a recognition of the world of meaning, a recognition of Those Who implement world affairs and Who engineer those steps which lead mankind onward towards its destined goal, plus a steadily increased recognition of the Plan on the part of the masses.

These three recognitions must be evidenced by humanity and affect human thinking and action if the total destruction of mankind is to be averted. They must form the theme of all the propaganda work to be done during the next few decades—until the year 2025—a brief space of time indeed to produce fundamental changes in human thought, awareness, and direction, but—at the same time— a quite possible achievement, provided the New Group of World Servers and the men and women of goodwill perform a conscientious task. Evil is not yet sealed.

The spread of the Christ consciousness and His recognised Presence with us is not yet attained. The Plan is not yet so developed that its structure is universally admitted. Evil has been driven back; there are enough people aware of the possibility of divine enlightenment and of the interdependence (which is the basis of love) to form a potent nucleus, provided again that the inertia so prevalent among spiritual people is overcome.

There is divine indication of coming events and a planned progress towards them, and this is already arousing interest among thinkers in many lands. However, the necessary responsive planning is still lacking."

Djwhal Khul, *Discipleship in the New Age Vol.2,* p. 164

As can be seen, Djwhal Khul makes a no-nonsense statement concerning the Decisions to be made at the Conclave in 2025 and the things humanity must do to avert destruction.

"1/. a recognition of the world of meaning

2/. a recognition of Those Who implement world affairs and Who engineer those steps which lead mankind onward towards its destined goal

3/. a steadily increased recognition of the Plan on the part of the masses."

Have we achieved this? If not, there are two major possibilities:

1/. Mankind is destroyed by some cataclysmic 'event'

or

2/ The World Teacher comes.

The World Teacher is expected very soon by all major religions and it is said the Kali Yuga comes to an end in 2025 (the age of quarrel and strife) and a new age begins. As we can clearly see 2025 is THE crunch time for humanity and only the Invocative cry of humanity can decide our fate. It should clearly be stated here that it is highly unlikely either event will take place exactly in 2025 as these things take decades to work through but it can be clearly stated that the decisions will be made.

"We have now the difficult task of considering an aspect of divine manifestation which is as yet so little apparent upon the physical plane that we lack the exact word with which to express it and those words available are likewise misleading. I can, however, attempt to give you certain concepts, relationships and parallels which may serve to close this section on astrology and lay a foundation for future teaching around the year 2025.

That is the mode whereby all revelation comes. A thought is given; a symbol described; an idea portrayed. Then, as the minds of men ponder upon it and the intuitives of the world pick up the thought, it serves as a seed thought which eventually comes to fruition with the presentation and the unfolding of a revelation which serves to lead the race of men nearer to their goal."

Djwhal Khul, *Esoteric Astrology,* p. 589

I believe that humanity has substantially lagged behind the intended progress that was outlined in the 1925 Conclave. There is no evidence of an outer World

Federation of Nations "taking rapid shape" nor much of the expected "stability":

"The inner structure of the World Federation of Nations will eventually be equally well organised, with its outer form taking rapid shape by 2025. Do not infer from this that we shall have a perfected world religion and a complete community of nations. Not so rapidly does nature move; but the concept and the idea will be universally recognised, universally desired, and generally worked for, and when these conditions exist nothing can stop the appearance of the ultimate physical form for that cycle."

Djwhal Khul, *Esoteric Psychology Vol.1,* p. 177

"This intensification of the light will continue until A.D. 2025, when there will come a cycle of relative stability and of steady shining without much augmentation. In the second decanate of Aquarius these three aspects will again be augmented by increased light from the fourth aspect, that is the light from the soul realm, reaching us via the universal "chitta" or mind stuff. This will flood the world. By that time, however, the soul will be recognised as a fact, and as a consequence of this recognition our entire civilisation will have changed so radically that we cannot today even guess at the form it will take.

Djwhal Khul, *Esoteric Psychology Vol.1,* p. 103

Again, Djwhal Khul makes it clear that 2025 is the year in which Maya/Glamour comes to its nadir and the tide is turned but, let's not forget, humanity has to meet the three conditions when the Stage of the Forerunner ends in 2025.

"I have made this practical application and the immediate illustration of the teaching anent glamour, illusion and maya because the whole world problem has reached a crisis today and because its clarification will be the outstanding theme of all progress—educational, religious and economic— until 2025 A.D."

Djwhal Khul, *Glamour: A World Problem,* p. 170

It was the Plan, agreed upon in 1925, that The Externalisation proper would start in 2025, that quite probably the date would be set for The World Teacher to Reappear and it could be in 2025 or within a decade or two of it. It is my view that this will be for a few reasons:

1/. That humanity has not achieved the Three Recognitions as planned

2/. That Intervention is needed

3/. That the invoking Call of the few will reach the Chamber's Ear

Only an Intervention will prevent the "if the total destruction of mankind is to be averted" scenario.

Djwhal Khul, the major spokesman for the Hierarchy post 1925, has made it clear that humanity will rise, succeed and grow no matter how long it may take. Despite the disappointment of humanities continual push to destroy our planet environmentally, politically and socially our eventual success is assured. Some believe that the war is won and see only goodness around others of us differ. This is the time for ACTION. It does not take many and we shall return to this theme later.

" These initiates exist in their thousands today; they will be present in their millions by the time the year 2025 arrives. All this re-orientation and unfoldment will be the result of the activity of the seventh ray and of the impact of its radiation upon humanity."

Djwhal Khul, *The Rays and The Initiations,* p. 571

In their "millions" by 2025 Djwhal Khul predicts. Has that happened? We don't really know but one might reasonably expect that this might have been delayed if humanity had not met the Three Recognitions as outlined and the World Federation had been delayed also. It is for each reader to judge for themselves if they think the Recognitions have been met, the World Federation will be in its outer form by 2025 and that there are millions of initiates in the world today.

"Thus, a great and new movement is proceeding and a tremendously increased interplay and interaction is taking place. This will go on until A.D. 2025. During the years intervening between now and then very great changes will be seen taking place, and at the great General Assembly of the Hierarchy—held as usual every century—in 2025 the date in all probability will be set for the first stage of the externalisation of the Hierarchy.

The present cycle (from now until that date) is called technically "The Stage of the Forerunner". It is preparatory in nature, testing in its methods, and intended to be revelatory in its techniques and results. You can see therefore that Chohans, Masters, initiates, world disciples, disciples and aspirants affiliated with the Hierarchy are all at this time passing through a cycle of great activity."

Djwhal Khul, *The Externalisation of the Hierarchy,* p. 530

"...hastening of certain plans which were slated (if I may use such a word) to take place several centuries later than this but which—owing to the unexpected preparedness of humanity—can take place, not prematurely really, but securely and in the fullness of time; this fullness of time, as regards the particular planning with which we are dealing, is from now until the year 2025 A.D."

Djwhal Khul, *The Externalisation of the Hierarchy,* p. 562

"...the tide of spiritual life has steadily flowed westward, and we may now look for a corresponding climax in the West, which will reach its zenith between the years 1965 and 2025."

Djwhal Khul, *The Light Of The Soul,* p. x

And lastly...

"...*A Treatise on Cosmic Fire*. This book was an expansion of the teaching given in *The Secret Doctrine* on the three fires—electric fire, solar fire and fire by friction—and it was an awaited sequence.

It also presented the psychological key to *The Secret Doctrine* and is intended to offer study to disciples and initiates at the close of this century and the beginning of the next century, up until 2025 A.D."

Alice A. Bailey, *The Unfinished Autobiography,* p. 246

The second part of the Great Teaching, *A Treatise on Cosmic Fire* was published as a result of the Convocation in 1925 and 2025 heralds the expected third part.

Will that be another set of books? Will it be the World Teacher? I suspect the latter. I also believe group work will totally overtake and replace work individually: Group Initiation, not individual.

Whatever happens, there will be great upheaval leading up to 2025 with huge environmental changes, magnetic activity (including the shifting of the Pole), disasters, political upheavals and wars. How will it end? Is this the "total destruction of humanity" on our doorstep? What Michael D. Robbins (University of the Seven Rays) when replying to a question anent World War Two, "I suspect worse could be on its way"

Can we stop it? How can we aid The World Teacher? Clear the path?

How do we change Djwhul Khul's "in all probability" into a PROBABILITY?

Djwhal Khul stated that it is a "quite possible achievement, provided the New Group of World Servers and the men and women of goodwill perform a conscientious task".

If it is "quite possible" then what must be done? If anything can it be individual work? Individuals, collectively can still make a change, using The Great Invocation is a powerful tool for humanity. I would suggest, as group work will be the work of the future that it is GROUP WORK that can have the greatest effect NOW.

Group work has, of course, been in progress for many decades through the work of Triangles and this has been the saviour of mankind. A network has been created and strengthened by this great work of thousands of people of Goodwill internationally. There is no doubt this has been one of the crowning achievements of mankind and sets the stage for the next, more focused, phase ahead.

Does it take "millions" to change the world? Actually, it doesn't. Individuals have changed our world on many levels let alone the great Avatars (World Teachers) who have been sent to aid and guide us. Individuals can change the world and groups, working in synthesis, can change the current dire potentiality of the world spinning into disaster in three ways:

1/. By working in synthesis to invoke the Coming of the World Teacher. By creating and sustaining the world antahkarana, the Rainbow Bridge of Light and as Djwhal Khul says:

"There are 'rainbow bridges' carrying the sevenfold energies of the seven rays from planet to planet, from system to system, and from plane to plane on cosmic levels."

Djwhal Khul, *The Rays and The Initiations,* p. 406

2/. By working to destroy negative thoughtforms through group action and focus

3/. By creating through group synthesis and discipline a Vortex/Funnel of energy that can be utilised by Hierarchy by using the OM:

"THE UNITED SOUNDING OF THE SACRED WORD.

This is one of the most usual methods, and the most direct way of forming a funnel for the transmission of power. If it is so effective in the case of the individual, as has been again and again demonstrated, surely its united use will be tremendously effective, and even dangerously potent."

Djwhal Khul, *Letters on Occult Meditation p.194*

Are there any groups active in this way? Joining the Triangle network through the Lucis Trust is highly recommended for individuals and groups of people who want to help the general work of Goodwill in the world.

A group that works in Twelve Formation, undertaking advanced esoteric work, was formed in the 1980s to undertake the first phase of experimental group work.

The first stage "Preparatory" was completed during 1999/2000 and the second stage "Implementory" was begun in 2019 and now has several Groups of Twelve in operation.

There is a third stage "Revelatory" which we currently have no knowledge about but assume is very much post 2025.

The first stage and the history of the group may be studied in this book the *Esoteric Apprentice*. Twelves is very much 2025 and beyond focused. Twelves also have a page on Facebook, search: "Twelves".

This work was also foretold by Master Morya in the book Agni Yoga:

"People do not wish to comprehend group action, which multiplies the forces. The dodecahedron is one of the most perfect formations; such a dynamic figure can resist many assaults. A group of Twelve men, systematically united, verily can master even cosmic events. It must be understood that enlarging of such a group can weaken it, destroying the dynamic force of its structure. Therefore you can notice Our formations of small groups."

Morya, *Agni Yoga* 1929 page 86

Morya

The group works in Twelve Formation to undertake the three devices to aid humanity as listed above. This work is currently done Distantly but it is planned that the group will meet physically. Physical Twelves were held for many years during the Preparatory stage in Europe and America.

Studying of Djwhal Khul's books is highly recommended, particularly His commentaries on future group work. All of His books are available through the Lucis Trust. Their full address and publishing details are listed page195.

Steven Chernikeeff

NOW is the time for earnest servers to come forth.

"For countless generations hath the adept built a fane of imperishable rocks, a giant's Tower of INFINITE THOUGHT , wherein the Titan dwelt, and will yet, if need be, dwell alone, emerging from it but at the end of every cycle, to invite the elect of mankind to cooperate with him and help in his turn to enlighten superstitious man. And we will go on in that periodical work of ours; we will not allow ourselves to be baffled in our philanthropic attempts until that day when the foundations of a new continent of thought are so firmly built that no amount of opposition and ignorant malice guided by the Brethren of the Shadow will be found to prevail."

Koot Hoomi, *'The Mahatma Letters to A.P.Sinnett Letter 9,* page 51

Koot Hoomi

And so we come to the zenith of human development, so far. The opportunity awaits each and every one of us. Shall we grasp it or turn away? Shall we engage or leave it to others? This is the hour that calleth all men and women to the Banner.

Let us hold it aloft honouring the thousands that have done so before us and in readiness for the thousands ahead of us.

"He who Beats upon the Door, then shall it be opened unto him.

He who sounds the Word, then shall he receive his answer"

The Initiate 1982

Chapter Eleven

———————◦◦———————

The Opportunity

WHAT IS esoteric meditation? Before we approach that let's discuss a little of meditation 101. Basically, there are two types of meditation that any of us can undertake. One, let's term it mystical meditation, is widely used and recognised under many names and is by and far the most popular.

Mystic meditation is based upon one actively trying to achieve a union with inner self or some higher power, God. It is useful for achieving a degree of oneness and is especially useful for mental and all-round health. It is practiced by most major religions and recommended by countless health practitioners.

In tandem with this form of meditation practitioners may add prayer, which gives it a service dimension and many groups exist to utilise prayer, with mystical meditation, as a form of service for world peace. Mystical meditation is reflective in nature and positive in outcome. It is an antidote to our material world and its stresses and, as has been suggested, can help with the work of goodwill and right human relations through prayer and invocation.

Most members of the New Group of World Servers (NGWS) utilise this form of meditation and many extrapolate it by linking in small groups of Triangles into a global grid. Most of these do it consciously, although the outcome is fairly passive, and some more experienced do add in an active element which brings it much closer to esoteric meditation.

As one becomes more experienced, and advances, the urge becomes a torrent and the quest to serve more actively becomes quintessentially one's guiding purpose. Why is this? There are two basic reasons. Firstly the Soul begins to gain control over the personality life and the student becomes more disciplined mentally, emotionally and physically. The result is the soul comes into more focused recognition of the need for service. Secondly the student comes into contact with his/her ashram, with the masters who serve there and hence a flow of connection is established and the mundane life cannot be returned to. Both these connections inspire one to further develop, take initiation and serve the ashram more closely.

The descriptions of the two forms are not resolute, of course, and there is cross-over. However, one is more passive and one overwhelmingly active. The discipline of mystical mediation improves us as individuals, clearing old karma, healing ourselves and through that healing, healing others and our world. Most esoteric meditation practitioners also undertake mystical meditation for the reasons outlined, but not together. Why is that? Esoteric meditation focuses on service, activity and clarity.

So, what is esoteric meditation? I have always noted the difference between prayer and invocation as being for self and for others and on a deeper level to a universal God and to a known focused source. I might say here, for clarity, that this is not necessarily widely accepted it is just helped me personally with the differential.

Djwhal Khul talked about The Great Invocation as a world prayer and so the definitions are not exact. I mention this point as I see the two differences of meditation output in a similar way. One, mostly, is for self-healing, union with God and inner peace. The other is, mostly, for service, focused and dynamic work with a specific outcome – often in groups, but not necessarily so, in groups all work is enhanced exponentially.

Esoteric meditation, then, is a service activity where a person consciously focuses his attention on undertaking work. Djwhal Khul work with Alice Bailey constantly emphasises group work and that the day of individuals working alone has passed.

The opportunity is for us to work in groups utilizing esoteric mediation as a focused tool for service. The Disciple balances the two approaches and their places are within the center ground.

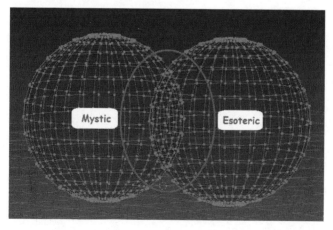

"If you will study the many books which I have written, you will discover that they have been basically occupied with the rules which govern the ability to do group work—which is the work to which the Hierarchy is eternally committed."

Djwhal Khul, *Discipleship in the New Age Vol.11*, p.237

"It is of importance that you realise that today something new is happening. There is the emergence of a new kingdom in nature, the fifth kingdom; this is the Kingdom of God on earth or the kingdom of souls. It is precipitating on earth and will be composed of those who are becoming group-conscious and who can work in group formation."

Djwhal Khul, *Discipleship in the New Age Vol.1*, p.3

"The word goes forth to the initiates of the future: Lose sight of self in group endeavour. Forget the self in group activity. Pass through the portal to initiation in group formation and let the personality life be lost in the group life."

Djwhal Khul, *The Externalisation of the Hierarchy*, p.41

Glossary

———◦———

Adept. A Master, or human being who, having traversed the path of evolution and entered upon the final stage of that path, the Path of Initiation, has taken five of the Initiations, and has therefore passed into the Fifth, or Spiritual kingdom, having but two more Initiations to take.

Agni Yoga. Teachings given by Master Morya principally through Helena Roerich (first book through Nicholas Roerich). Accepted by most esotericists as one of the three great streams of teachings (so far).

Angel. (or Deva). A god. In Sanskrit a resplendent deity. An Angel is a celestial being, whether good, bad, or indifferent. Angels are divided into many groups, and are called not only angels and archangels, but lesser and greater builders.

Archeometre. A twelve-sided instrument used by ancients to aid understanding esoteric truths.

Ashram. The centre to which the Master gathers the disciples and aspirants for personal instruction and service work.

Aspirant. One who has chosen to step onto the pathway but not yet taken the First Initiation.

Astral bell (or Gong). Often heard when Helena Blavatsky visited people. Ethereal and said to be heard 'behind the silence' in meditation the bell is some sort of 'homing' device on the inner planes. It could be related to one's ashram but, largely, it remains a mystery.

Aura. A subtle invisible essence or fluid which emanates from human and animal bodies, and even from things. It is a psychic effluvium, partaking of both mind and body. It is electro-vital, and also electro-mental.

Bodhisattva. Literally, he whose consciousness has become intelligence, or buddhi. Those who need but one more incarnation to become perfect buddhas. As used in these letters the Bodhisattva is the name of the office which is at present occupied by the Lord Maitreya, Who is known in the Occident as the Christ. This office might be translated as that of World Teacher. The Bodhisattva is the Head of all the religions of the world, and the Master of the Masters and the Teacher of angels and of men.

Buddha (The). The name given to Gautama. Born in India about B.C. 621, he became a full buddha in B.C. 592. The Buddha is one who is the "Enlightened" and has attained the highest degree of knowledge possible for man in this solar system.

Causal Body. This body is, from the standpoint of the physical plane, no body, either subjective or objective. It is, nevertheless, the centre of the egoic consciousness, and is formed of the conjunction of buddhi and manas. It is relatively permanent and lasts throughout the long cycle of incarnations, and is only dissipated after the fourth initiation, when the need for further rebirth on the part of a human being no longer exists.

Deva (or Angel). A god. In Sanskrit a resplendent deity. A Deva is a celestial being, whether good, bad, or indifferent. Devas are divided into many groups, and are called not only angels and archangels, but lesser and greater builders.

Disciple. One who has been accepted into the ashram of a Master.

*Djwhal Khul (*DK*).* Also known as 'The Tibetan' he first appeared in Helena Blavatsky's work and then later he used Alice A. Bailey as his recorder for the blue books which are the backbone of modern esotericism and a continuation of Blavatsky's work for the masters.

Elementals. The Spirits of the Elements; the creatures involved in the four kingdoms, or elements, Earth, Air, Fire, and Water. Except a few of the higher kinds and their rulers they are forces of nature more than ethereal men and women.

Etheric body. (Etheric double.) The physical body of a human being is, according to occult teaching, formed of two parts, the dense physical body, and the etheric body. The dense physical body is formed of matter of the lowest three subplanes of the physical plane. The etheric body is formed of the four highest or etheric subplanes of the physical plane.

Hierarchy. That group of spiritual beings on the inner planes of the solar system who are the intelligent forces of nature, and who control the evolutionary processes. They are themselves divided into **Twelve Hierarchies**. Within our planetary scheme, the earth scheme, there is a reflection of this Hierarchy which is called by the occultist the Occult Hierarchy. This Hierarchy is formed of chohans, masters, adepts, and initiates working through their disciples, and, by this means, in the world.

Initiate. From the Latin root meaning the first principles of any science. One who is penetrating the mysteries of the science of the Self and of the oneself in all selves. The Path of Initiation is the final stage of the path of evolution trodden by man, and is divided into five stages, called the Five Initiations. At the fifth the Initiate becomes a Master.

Karma. Physical action. Metaphysically, the law of retribution; the law of cause and effect, or ethical causation. There is the karma of merit and the karma of demerit. It is the power that controls all things, the resultant of moral action, or the moral effect of an act committed for the attainment of something which gratifies a personal desire.

Krishnamurti. Was identified at an early age to become the physical vehicle for Christ and the Order of the Star organisation was built to prepare both Krishnamurti and the world for His Coming.

Koot Hoomi. Working firstly with H.P.Blavatsky then Alice A. Bailey, Master Koot Hoomi is Head of the Second Ray.

Logos. The deity manifested through every nation and people.

Maya. Sanskrit, "Illusion." Of the principle of form or limitation. The result of manifestation. Generally used in a relative sense for phenomena or objective appearances that are created by the mind.

Morya. Working firstly with H.P.Blavatsky then Alice A. Bailey, Master Morya is Head of the First Ray.

Organons. Groups of nine people who work in unison for assistance to the hierarchy.

Quaternary. The fourfold lower self, or man, in the three worlds. There are various divisions of this, but perhaps for our purpose the best is to enumerate the four as follows:

1. Lower mind.

2. Emotional or kamic body.

3. Prana, or the Life Principle.

4. The etheric body, or the highest division of the twofold physical body.

Ray. One of the seven streams of force of the Logos; the seven great lights. Each of them is the embodiment of a great cosmic entity. The seven Rays can be divided into the three Rays of Aspect and the four Rays of Attribute, as follows:

Rays of Aspect

1. The Ray of Will, or Power.

2. The Ray of Love-Wisdom.

3. The Ray of Activity or Adaptability.

Rays of Attribute

4. The Ray of Harmony, Beauty, Art, or Unity.

5. The Ray of Concrete Knowledge or Science.

6. The Ray of Abstract Idealism or Devotion.

7. The Ray of Ceremonial Magic, or Law.

The Disciples Invocation. Released in the 1980s specifically for use with the Twelves Formation.

The Great Invocation. Released in 1945 as the primary tool for all of humanity. The Great Invocation is a world Invocation translated into over 80 languages and dialects.

The Twelves Group. Working in a group formation of twelve people to assist Hierarchy in specific ways (i.e. energy work etc.).

Wesak. A festival which takes place in the Himalayas at the full moon of April/May (esoterically Taurus but celebrated by Buddhists at the full moon of May). It is said that at this festival, at which all the members of the Hierarchy are present, the Buddha, for a brief period, renews his touch and association with the work of our planet.

Adapted from: Alice A. *Bailey Letters on Occult Meditation* with additional material.

Works Cited

Achad, Frater

The Anatomy of the Body of God

Phoenix: Collegium ad Spiritum Sanctum, 1925

Bailey, Alice A.

A Treatise on White Magic

New York: Lucis Publishing Company, 1925

Discipleship in the New Age Vol.1

New York: Lucis Publishing Company, 1944

Discipleship in the New Age II.

New York: Lucis Publishing Company, 1955

Esoteric Psychology I

New York: Lucis Publishing Company, 1936

Esoteric Psychology II

New York: Lucis Publishing Company, 1942

Glamour a World Problem

New York: Lucis Publishing Company, 1950

The Light of the Soul: Its Science and Effect: a paraphrase of the Yoga Sutras of Patanjali.

New York: Lucis Publishing Company, 1955

The Destiny of the Nations.

New York: Lucis Publishing Company, 1949

Letters on Occult Meditation

New York: Lucis Publishing Company, 1922

The Externalisation of the Hierarchy

New York: Lucis Publishing Company, 1957

The Rays and Initiations

New York: Lucis Publishing Company, 1960

Esoteric Astrology

New York: Lucis Publishing Company, 1951

Esoteric Healing

New York: Lucis Publishing Company, 1953.

Blavatsky, H. P.

ISIS Unveiled

Adyar: The Theosophical Publishing House, 1877

Barker, A.T.

The Mahatma Letters to A.P.Sinnett

London: T.Fisher Unwin, 1923

Chevalier , Jean and Gheerbrant, Alain *The Penguin Dictionary of Symbols* London: Penguin Books, 1969

Corlot , J.E.

A Dictionary of Symbols

New York: Dover Publications, 1962

Ellis, George F. R.

The Shape of the Universe

London: Nature Magazine Vol 425, October 9, 2003

Hall, Manly P.

The Secret Teachings of the Ages

Los Angeles: The Philosophical Research Society, 1928

Menog i Xrad

The Zoroastrian Book

London: Manuscript British Library, 1520

Plato

The Republic

London: Penguin Classics, 2007

Plutarch

Delphi Complete Works

East Sussex: Delphi Publishing, 2013

Roerich, Helena

Agni Yoga

New York: Agni Yoga Society, 1929

Roberts, Ursula

Hints on Spiritual Unfoldment

Privately published by Ursula Roberts, 1964

Saint-Yves d'Alveydre, Marquis

The Archeometre and Oriental Tradition

Santa Barbara: Sacred Science Institute, 2008

Sinclair, John

The Other Universe

London: Rider, 1973

About the Author

Steven was born in London of a Russian father and English mother.

He retired early from a successful career in management in the UK and now lives a fairly solitary life in Asia with his cat Yin.

Outside of the esoteric field Steven enjoys travelling, nature and movies.

Reviews

"The Esoteric Apprentice is a special book that makes an important contribution to the understanding of esoteric practice when it is aimed at human and planetary betterment. The work in question, Twelves, concerns, in layperson's terms, a form of ritualised group meditation.

Chernikeeff provides insights into the motivations, purpose or intention, the methods and the reasoning behind pure, spiritually focused group work, which serves to put into practice that which was delineated at considerable length in the texts of Theosophist Alice A. Bailey. Written as memoir in accessible and engaging prose, the narrative is peppered with explanations and quotations, providing the lay reader with a sort of primer, and the esoterically minded with an example of what is achievable through dedication and a commitment to act.

Chernikeeff documents twenty years of dedication and commitment in a very human manner. Honesty, integrity and above all humility infuse this short book. The structure and presentation are excellent. Alice Bailey's texts were meant not only to inform and help foster inner transformation, they were given as guidance for esoteric practice in all its forms, for the use by those on the right-hand path of love, wisdom and goodwill.

Chernikeeff and the Twelves participants are to be commended for their efforts at applying the teachings, captured by the author in The Esoteric Apprentice. In all, The Esoteric Apprentice is a valuable resource and a must read for all esoteric practitioners who aspire to foster global change for the better."

Isobel Blackthorn, author *The Unlikely Occultist* (a novel about Alice A. Bailcy), *Clarissa's Warning, A Matter of Latitude* and many others.

Isobel, a member of Twelves, is currently writing a full Biography of Alice A. Bailey.

"It was with great pleasure that I read Steven's book a book I had been looking forward to. There are very few books like it in the esoteric field. Almost a hundred years ago the Tibetan teacher Djwhal Khul began giving information on the imminent and momentous "Externalization of the Hierarchy."

In Christian terms this is the establishment of the "Kingdom of God" on Earth, composed of those who are living and functioning as souls(characterized by love and wisdom), of which there are now millions throughout the world. The Tibetan teaches that the Soul is not only a higher consciousness, but a higher spiritual energy, and that this energy, transmitted by disciples and initiates, plays a key role in transforming humanity.

One of the major contributions of the Tibetan was the inauguration of meditation groups with a focus on service using "occult" meditation the conscious invocation and distribution of spiritual energies. We are told that disciples in such groups are brought together by unseen forces for such work. This requires knowledge, a fairly advanced spiritual development, but also a special connection between the individuals in such a group involving a deep unity of soul, heart and purpose.

In Steven's group, a unique and rare opportunity existed where it was possible for them to become an active vehicle for the spiritual forces generated by much greater beings than they had ever before been conscious of. And that is indeed what Steven documents.

Naturally these advanced specialized groups are relatively few, though they have greatly increased over the last Century. They are truly "seed groups." And Steven's account is a rare glimpse into such a pioneering seed group.

The first thing that impressed me reading Steven's account is that his experience is a confirmation of the "externalization" process itself as well as certain predictions Master DK made regarding esoteric groups. The Masters and initiates are indeed engaged in this process and actively guiding their chosen ones, as they did with Steven and the "Groups of Twelve." His group received direct teachings from an initiate new information required for their esoteric work but in perfect harmony with what had previously been given (through Alice A. Bailey and a few others).

This new information in Steven's book is certainly one of its most important contributions to the esoteric field and is of great value to future generations."

Patrick Chouinard, esotericist, teacher and author

"Steven Chernikeeff's book *The Esoteric Apprentice* is a captivating personal recount of an occult experiment in group work consciously aligned with a group of Masters on the inner planes.

Their group received instruction to undertake work in twelve formation and to act as a conduit for Hierarchical ashramic energy, as an experiment of the triangles work undertaken by Lucis Trust and others. The method of teaching was given through higher telepathy during their ashramic meditation. It described an experiment in founding or starting focal points in the human family through which certain energies can flow out into the entire race of men. A profound and fascinating read, highly recommended."

Stephane Chollet, CEO Surya World, teacher and esotericist

"*The Esoteric Apprentice* offers a fascinating look into the world of inner group work and meditation, the challenges involved in group co-operation and working in the subtle realms.

There is much value here for newcomers to group meditation, the pitfalls involved and the joy of group service."

Phillip Lindsay, author *Unveiling Genesis, The Initiations of Krishnamurti,* etc.

"I have just this moment completed reading *The Esoteric Apprentice* first reading, taken over a period of 2-3 days reading a chapter or two in a session.

I simply must tell you how deeply touched I am with your very clear, heartfelt, forthrightly honest communication of your (and the Group's) journey with what became Twelves Group work.

Chapter 7 is the most significant chapter for me on a personal basis. I am deeply, deeply touched by what you have conveyed in that Chapter to the point of tears.

Thank you, thank you, thank you for this very important book."

Shizandra Goodwin, an original member of Twelves in the 1990s and now back working with Twelves in the Implementation Stage.

"Excellent Esoteric Review

This book presents a very clear and concise Path to a viable esoteric service. It offers hope and instruction rarely found today."

Kindle Customer

"I have been involved with Theosophy and Esotericism for a long time and a student of Alice Bailey's books especially and have come across many groups that assist this work internationally. I was astounded to read of the group described in this small book as I have no knowledge of it.

They take the work of DK and Alice Bailey and expand it from threes to groups of twelves. They actually did this physically, in group sessions, and I find the concept astounding. This has the real potential to expand into a world service work of great import. They also had direct contact with the Spiritual Hierarchy (or one of its members) guiding them through the process.

Read the reviews on this page and if you want to know what it is really like to serve within a group setting get this book."

Salvator Mundi, Amazon Customer

"I have just completed this book and I am quiet taken aback.

I have read DK's books for many decades and have been one of the excited thousands waiting for the externalization to be seen here on earth. I was staggered to read that a group had actually taken DK's material and put it into ritual practice. I had no idea that such a group existed or about the work in twelves as foretold by Master M. in the book Agni Yoga and DK in the 24 books with Alice Bailey.

It was a thrill to read this group met and worked together in harmony to bring light and love to our world and this was predicted by DK and M. I do wish this work was continuing today and I can only assume this sets a kind of template for the future?

Bravo! to all of you who joined in and how lucky you were."

Susan, Goodreads

"Students of the esoteric realm understand not only the importance but the necessity of group work for the future of humanity. *The Esoteric Apprentice* is an account of some who responded to the call and worked as a group for 20 years. From the first GONG until the eventual dissipation of this group, we can learn much. As each of us plays a role, however small, in the lives and future of all, it is my hope that more groups form and undertake the service that lies ahead. Kudos Steven for your service and for bringing this concept more into the light!"

Mindy Burge, healer, esotericist and core member of Twelves.

"Inspiring experience for all who wish to make a difference in the world.

Excellent explanation of the beauty and challenges one might expect in performing group work of an esoteric nature. The book is easy to read, written from the Heart and with humility, with profound insight into the ways we can join forces with others to bring about collective healing when entered into with sincerity and love. I highly recommend Steven's book and encourage participation within your community in whatever capacity you are called to do."

Silvia Pancaro, astrologer

"This book is a very new and intriguing, behind the curtain examination of an extremely rare venture. It feels incredibly special to get a glimpse of the work undertaken by this inspiring group and the fact the first meeting took place in Glastonbury, only a stone's throw away from where I live, makes it all the more outstanding. I've read Alice Bailey's books, and this expands on her work in a very exciting way. Definitely a must read!"

Kelly, Goodreads

"Having read many books by Bailey, Besant, Blavatsky, Steiner and Hall, I looked forward to reading *The Esoteric Apprentice* by Steven Chernikeeff. How exciting that their group of Twelve was doing this work and I hope others are able to assume the mantle. A must read for other Theosophists."

Kylah Peterman, Goodreads

"This book presents a very clear and concise Path to a viable esoteric service. It offers hope and instruction rarely found today."

Katherine D, Goodreads

Alice A. Bailey's books are available from:

Lucis Trust, Suite 54, 3 Whitehall Court, London SW1A 2EF UK

www.lucistrust.org

Addendum

Concerning Krishnamurti and the original World Teacher experiment

(a paper submitted to the esoteric community in 2019)

<hr/>

Krishnamurti: The Dissolution, an Alternative View

By Steven Chernikeeff MSc, MA

"I maintain truth is a pathless land"[1]

August 3rd, 1929

And with those words the young Jiddu Krishnamurti (affectionately known as K.) drifted off into his nihilist (with love K. style of course) new life. The most common view is that K. rejected the role of vehicle for The World Teacher, rejected his dearest friends in the TS and thenceforth rejected the whole canon of teaching from Abraham to Zarathusa.

Many of my Theosophical friends dismissively claim, "K. rejected The World Teacher" and that was, as they say, that. This, I must confess, is the widely held view of most esoteric students who accept K.'s Order of the Star dissolution speech at Ommen in 1929 but then, miraculously, accept Djwhal Khul's announcement through is amanuensis Alice A. Bailey (AAB):

The "Point of Decision" … during the Full Moon of June, 1936, and the Full Moon of June 1945… it resulted in the decision arrived at by the Christ* to reappear or return to visible Presence on Earth as soon as possible" [2]

(i.e. physically without need for a vehicle such as K.)

*I would contend that this decision was, in all likelihood, originally taken at the 1925 one-hundred-year Conclave, but not as to exact timing which was decided 1936 to 1945. This is open to debate but is not a major concern for this paper.

Without going through all the known history of where K. was discovered, why and by whom let us dwell, albeit a short while, upon K.'s relationship to the ashram the Brotherhood of the Star, it's outer reflection The Order of the Star and the Master Koot Hoomi (KH). It is said that K. took the First Initiation in 1911 when he was out of his body for 3 days. [3]

Just before that K. had published in 1910 his book At The feet of The Master [4] which was dictated to him by KH in his sleep.

It didn't stop there. K. was intimately engaged with leading The Order of the Star from 1911 until its dissolution (which we will alight upon again later) in 1929. Writing many books, lectures and attending huge camps the Order had 100,000 members and many prominent supporters. Modern K. theorists try to dismiss this part of K.'s life as early or immature and, mostly, do not even mention it.

There is much evidence that K. was as absorbed, and accepted his role in The Coming as much as those surrounding him:

"I would ask you, as a members of the Star, who believe in the Coming, who know what it means to breathe the same air as He does, who know what it means to look at the same sunshine as He does, who enjoy the same flower as He does... I saw my Happiness, my Guru, my Teacher, the Teacher of every one of us walking towards me." [5]

As can be seen K. makes mention of meeting The World Teacher and this happened on many occasions and on many occasions, K. was overshadowed for quite long periods. K. fully accepted his role, in the same fashion as Jesus did as vehicle for the same Great Being we know in the West as Christ, the East as Maitreya, the Bodhisattva and the Iman Mahdi but a more inclusive term "The World Teacher".

"When the Teacher is here, we are all going to be near Him. We are going to drink in the beauty and the glory, and we are going to try and understand thoroughly everything that He will say. That is where the thrill comes, of being able to be forerunners." [6]

Interesting that the Stage of the Forerunner ends in 2025. [7] Unrelated, maybe, but an interesting turn of phrase from K. I think it is obvious, then, that we discard the first yearning from K.'s detractors that he was manipulated or did not take part as he assuredly did take part and lead The Order of the Star and accept his role as vehicle as I have demonstrated.

My intention is to set out that there is an alternative view of K.'s dissolution of The Order of the Star that bears little relation to the popularized one that he gave up or rejected the Masters. If we just observed K.'s writings and the press of the day I do accept that the former view would be taken as fact but little in the esoteric genre can be taken at face value. We are to observe, question and examine not just accept because someone says it. I only ask that we apply this basic premise to K. and The Dissolution.

Another thing to note is that in 1925 Nitya, K.'s brother, died. It has been recorded that K. had asked the masters to intervene and save his brother and that this request was granted. Alas Nitya died. K. was devastated and never fully recovered. K. ranted and raved that the masters had let him down. [8]

The Hierarchy met at the 100 year Conclave and, I submit, in all likelihood, made the decision that the experiment could not succeed and the initial decision, which might not have been the culminating, final decision, was made that The World Teacher would return utilising His own vehicle and that the decision to repeat the successful Christ via Jesus (The World Teacher via a chosen vehicle) model could not be repeated.

The fact that K. could not fill the role should bring no shame in its stead. Times have changed, K. had the delusions and Messianic devotion to deal with and this, ultimately, is what ended the Greatest Experiment of that century. K. was a third degree initiate very close to taking the 4th (as was Jesus although it is generally accepted Jesus was more advanced). From the Conclave decision in 1925, and the enormous energy shift that brought, K. questioned the masters on many occasions and appeared to value being increasingly vague concerning them.

What is very clear and is indisputable is that K. from 1925, until the dissolution of the Order of the Star in 1929, had changed and that those around him sensed and felt that change. This period was one of growing disillusion in his teachers, his organisation and the future that had been mapped out for him.

As I have stated it is my proposition that The World Teacher, and the Hierarchy, had decided that K. was not able to fulfil his mission as Vehicle and it was THAT that led to K.'s apparent decision to dissolve the Order four years later.

It might seem of academic interest only, but it is important to note the difference as it highlights that:

It was not K.'s decision

It sheds light on why K. became disillusioned from 1925 onwards

It explains why The World Teacher announced returning Himself

It helps to understand the subsequent Alice A. Bailey collaboration

And so, I write this partly to clarify for my ashramic senior brother K. and to be a counterweight to those who enjoy blaming K. for the failure and, for those, who might never have questioned or challenged the accepted narrative. Even amongst those brothers whom I highly respect brother K. gets the Lion's share of the blame and I hope some might ponder that this is a little unfair.

The withdrawal of The World Teacher's energy would have been enormously disruptive and disturbing, and it took many years for this process to work through. As we know K. went on to develop his own specialized teaching through 200 books over many decades. K. always retained a fondness, or love even, for his old mentors at the Theosophical Society returning to Adyar in the 1980s

"When Mrs Radha Burnier became President of the Theosophical Society in 1980, Krishnamurti began to visit Adyar, where he had spent many memorable years. Four and a half decades had passed before that day on 3

November 1980 when he again visited the Headquarters of the Theosophical Society, where he was warmly welcomed. He walked through the grounds to the Adyar beach followed by a throng of people.

Again, in December during the Theosophical Convention he met the delegates and visited Dr Besant's room and the apartment she had built for him. In the following years, Krishnamurti regularly visited Adyar whenever he was in Chennai and took a walk on the beach. During the last years of his life, he was often heard speaking about Annie Besant's greatness, love and understanding." [9]

It might be debated whether the K. experiment was part of the first stage or second stage of the teachings to be given to humanity as outlined by DK through Alice Bailey but the one thing we do know is that the work of AAB and DK was the second stage and we await the third 'sometime after AD 2025' [10] (when if certain conditions are met the Externalisation of the Hierarchy begins – but in any case the Stage of the Forerunner ends and The World Teacher is expected from 2025 onwards).

DK makes mention of K.'s teachings post 1929 as K. worked through his own development and preparation for the fourth initiation:

"What is the immediate revelation which the initiates and the disciples of the world are seeking to bring to humanity? What aspect of this essential unity are they endeavouring to make simple and apparent? One of the easiest things in the world to say (as has, for instance, Krishnamurti) is that life is one; that there is nothing but unity. That is a trite formulation of a very ancient truth, and one which is today an occult platitude." [11]

To end on a quotation from DK that seems to support the proposition that the Hierarchy, of which Christ is a member, ended the K. experiment which They started:

"One of the first experiments He made as He prepared for this form of activity was in connection with Krishnamurti. It was only partially successful. The power used by Him was distorted and misapplied by the devotee type of which the Theosophical Society is largely composed, and the experiment was brought to an end: it served, however, a most useful purpose. As a result of the war, mankind has been disillusioned; devotion is no longer regarded as adequate or necessary to the spiritual life or its effectiveness. The war was won, not through devotion or the attachment of millions of men to some prized ideal; it was won by the simple performance of duty, and the desire to safeguard human rights. Few men were heroes, as the newspapers stupidly proclaim. They were drafted and taught to fight and had to fight. It was a group recognition of duty. When Christ again seeks to overshadow His disciples, a different reaction will be looked for. It is because of this that A.A.B. has so consistently belittled devotion and advocated spiritual independence. No devotee is independent; he is a prisoner of an idea or a person." [12]

Note:

"the experiment was brought to an end"

I offer you the suggestion that this wording "brought to an end" implies not a decision of K.'s but a decision made by Hierarchy and The World Teacher in 1925 at the 100-year Conclave and worked through in 1936 to 1945.

Addendum
Works Cited

[1] Lutyens, Lady Emily , *Candles in the Sun* (London: Rupert Hart-Davies, 1957, p. 173)

[2] Bailey, Alice A., *The Reappearance of The Christ* (New York, Lucis Publishing Company, 1948, p. 69)

[3] Lutyens, Lady Emily, *Candles in the Sun* (London: Rupert Hart-Davies, 1957, p. 28)

[4] Krishnamurti, Jiddu, *At the Feet of The Master* (Adyar, Theosophist Office, 1910)

[5] Krishnamurti, Jiddu, *The Pool of Wisdom* (Ommen, The Star Publishing Trust, 1927, pp. 28/30)

[6] Krishnamurti, Jiddu, *Towards Discipleship* (Chicago, The Theosophical Press, 1926, p. 77)

[7] Bailey, Alice A., *The Externalisation of the Hierarchy* (New York, Lucis Publishing Company, 1957, p. 530)

[8] Vernon, Roland, *Star in the East* (London, Constable, 2000, p. 152)

[9] Nilakanta, Subha, Talk delivered on Adyar Day, 17 February 2003.

[10] Bailey, Alice A., *The Externalisation of the Hierarchy* (New York, Lucis Publishing Company, 1957, p. 530)

[11] Bailey, Alice A., *Rays and the Initiations* (New York, Lucis Publishing Company, 1960, p. 299/300)

[12] Bailey, Alice A., *Discipleship in the New Age, Vol 11*, (New York, Lucis Publishing Company, 1955, pp. 171/172)

Made in the USA
Middletown, DE
20 November 2020